Other books by Graham Sutherland

Dastardly Deeds in Victorian Warwickshire
Leamington Spa, a photographic history of your Town
Leamington Spa, Francis Frith's Town & City Memories
Around Warwick, Francis Frith's Photographic Memories
Knights of the Road
Warwick Chronicles 1806-1812
Warwick Chronicles 1813-1820
Felons, Phantoms & Fiends
North to Alaska
Taste of Ale
Bloody British History – Warwick
Warwick in the Great War
Warwick at War 1939-45

Fiction:
Mayfield
Mayfield's Law
Mayfield's Last Case
Conspiracy of Fate
To Kill The King

Short Stories
Old Cavendish and other Supernatural Stories

In preparation:
Sleepers Awake

*This book is dedicated to all those
amazing people who enabled our country to
keep going throughout the Covid-19
crisis in 2020/2021.
From all those involved in the NHS,
to shopkeepers, social workers, police officers,
carers, delivery drivers, refuse collectors
and everybody else, and other unsung heroes
who have helped us get through these
terrible times… I salute you all.*

WICKED, WILFUL AND UNCONVENTIONAL WOMEN

Graham Sutherland

KNOWLE VILLA BOOKS

About the Author

Graham Sutherland is a retired police inspector, married with three adult daughters and two granddaughters. He has lived in Warwick for more than forty years where, until 2014, he was beadle and town crier.

He is a Blue Badge tourist guide for the Heart of England Region, with special interests in Warwick, Royal Leamington Spa, Stratford-upon-Avon, Oxford and the Cotswolds.

A keen historian, he gives numerous talks each year, mainly on social and crime related topics. At one time he was secretary of the Warwickshire Constabulary History Society, where he developed a special interest in policing during Victorian and Edwardian Times.

For more information about Graham, please visit his website

www.talksandwalks.co.uk

or visit him on Facebook.

Contents

Words and terms presented
in **bold italics** reference an entry in the
Glossary presented on
pages 210-222 when they first appear
in every account.

Introduction

Before starting a study of wicked, wilful and unconventional women, it is necessary to establish just what is meant by these words. Here are a few suggestions, but there is no singular definition for any one of them.

Wicked has been described as: Bad in moral character, disposition or conduct: Inclined or addicted to wilful wrong: Morally depraved: Of bad quality or cruel.

Wilful can be applied to persons doing something which is bad, harmful, headstrong, stubborn, strong-willed and generally changing their behaviour in a way which is difficult to control: all with the intention of doing what they want to do regardless of the consequences

Unconventional is acting in a manner which is contrary to what is normally expected of them. It can be argued how like beauty, these definitions lie in the eye of the beholder. Many historical records tend to be biased, one way or the other, depending on the writer`s viewpoint, and how scandalous the crimes or misdeeds were.

In the author`s younger days as a police officer, newspaper reports of incidents he had attended sometimes appeared. Having read them, he often found they bore little or no resemblance to what had really happened and wondered if it was the same incident. A story had been made up around the facts. Eye catching headlines are nothing new and not all court records have survived over the years and newspaper and other reports may be the only source of information.

For instance, in the Bancroft Gardens, at Stratford-upon-Avon, there is a statue of William Shakespeare, surrounded by four characters, each one representing a different type of his plays. One is Lady Macbeth, who represents tragedy. If you believe Shakespeare, she was a particularly evil woman, who manipulated her husband, and was probably one of the wickedest women ever to have lived. But was she?

Macbeth was written in early 1606, very soon after the failure of the Gunpowder Plot. As James I of England maintained one of his ancestors, Banquo, was allegedly murdered by the Macbeths, there was no way they were going to get a good press from him. Remember too, Shakespeare was a dramatist and not an historian.

Another example would be the suffragettes, at the latter end of the nineteenth and early twentieth centuries. They would be regarded as sinners or saints, depending on how you saw them. Queen Victoria, for instance, did not approve of them. She considered their aims to be a '*mad wicked folly*.'

In other examples, it may be the so-called sinners were more sinned against, than being the outright villains of the piece. Women had very little say or influence in most legal, financial and property matters, until the latter part of the nineteenth century and in the post-war period from 1919. Regardless of how many of the following characters were wicked or not, the author suggests they were all unconventional to some degree. Sometimes by choice, but also by force of circumstances. Undoubtedly some were just good time girls.

At least one was possibly more of an eccentric with the advantage of having money. Most eccentrics tended to be males because until the **Married Women's Property Act 1870**, they were the only ones with money. There is a fine dividing line between eccentricity and insanity. If you have the money, you are an eccentric. But if you do not …you fall into the other category.

We need to remember how until 1898 in English Law defendants were not permitted to testify on oath. They had to rely on lawyers who chose to act on their behalf. The courts believed it was better for an innocent person to hang than for a guilty one to escape by committing perjury and thereby imperiling their immortal souls. Evidence on oath tends to be better received by juries, who may attach more weight to it in preference to a non-sworn or affirmed statement. There was no Court of Criminal Appeal until 1907.

It is easy to examine these cases in the twenty-first century and criticize the way they were conducted. But the burden of proof was not so particular and police investigation was nothing like what it is today. The first official female to sit on an English jury did so in 1920 and there were no majority verdicts until 1967.

One thing remains paramount in all murder cases. The Crown, (i.e. the Prosecution) has to prove:

Motive…Means…and…Opportunity in all cases. It is not a question of choice. ALL THREE points have to be proved. If not, then the defendant must be given the benefit of the doubt and be acquitted. Although Scottish law has some differences, these three points still apply.

The following are just a selection of some of the more better-known and perhaps not so well-known women who became infamous by murders or scandals.

It is a general observation how poison is mainly a woman`s weapon on the premise they do not possess the necessary physical strength or courage to use more violent measures. This observation is true to a degree, but men have also used poisons. For decades poison had been very easy to acquire and signing the poisons register made very little difference to any illegal usage.

Whilst readers may be divided about the wicked or wilful, question, there can be little doubt they were all unconventional. However, what was unconventional years ago, is not necessarily so today.

The acid test, the author suggests, for deciding if these women were wicked and/or wilful is quite simple.

Would you or would you not want to have them as your daughter-in-law? Might you want to think twice about going to have a meal with some of them?

The decision is yours.

Note:

1. I have endeavoured to show dates of birth and death, but in some cases I am unable to do so and question marks have been inserted and only the dates of the offences and/or trial or shown. e.g. (?-1899/1900-?)

2. There are several Warwickshire cases as this book was created following a presentation I gave, on Wicked Warwickshire Women.

3. Wherever possible I have used locations as they would have been when these events happened, and not where they are situated today.

4. The added modern day values came from the Currency Converter Programme on the Internet.

5. For ease of reading and to avoid continual repetition of recurring themes such as poisons, I have included them and other definitions in a glossary at the end of the book between Kate Webster and acknowledgements.

1

Mary Ball *née Ward* (?1818-1849)

Mary Ball has the dubious distinction of being the last person to be publicly executed in Coventry. Although hanged here, she lived in nearby Nuneaton, Warwickshire, where the crime was committed.

She had married Thomas Ball in 1837, and it is fair to say, they had a stormy relationship. During this time, Mary had borne six children, only one of whom survived.

On 18th May 1849, after one of their regular stormy shouting matches, Thomas left home and went fishing. He had not been home very long, when he experienced severe stomach pains and went to bed. Medical advice, such as was available, was obtained and Thomas was diagnosed as suffering from a bowel inflammation.

Next morning, his fishing companion of the previous day, Joseph Petty visited and found Thomas in agony. The man was being sick and unable to urinate. Thomas later complained about his arms being numb and felt certain he was going to die. Joseph said Mary sat crying in another room.

Early the following morning, she roused Joseph and said '*Tom's dead.*'

The doctor gave the cause of death as the result of a stomach complaint with what he loosely described as complications. So far so good, but then matters began to unravel as one of Mary's neighbours sat with her. Imagine her surprise when Mary said how glad she was that Tom was dead. In a very short time, her comments soon became the topic of local gossip and people remembered certain other incidents.

They recalled her shouting after Tom on several occasions and threatening to poison him. Another remembered being with Mary when she purchased some **arsenic**, supposedly for killing rats. On the way home, Mary had asked if it was enough to kill a man. The neighbours asked what had she done with the arsenic. Her reply was she had mixed it in a cup and then threw it down a hole. When the hole was searched, no trace of any cup was found.

With suspicions running high, rumours began about there being a *post-mortem*. Mary panicked and started asking what had happened to the unused arsenic which she had left on the mantelpiece? Might Tom have taken it thinking the powder was *Epsom Salts*, thereby being poisoned by mistake.

There was a post-mortem and Mary's worst fears were realized when arsenic was found in his stomach. Her arrest and being charged with her husband's murder soon followed. She was taken to Coventry and imprisoned in the city gaol until her trial there on 28 July 1849 at the Summer Assizes.

As can well be imagined, with so much notoriety already circulating about the case, the venue at County Hall was besieged by the ghoulish crowds such a trial attracted. When the charge was put to her, Mary pleaded not guilty and the trial began.

Her counsel took nearly two hours for his summing up and the judge took twenty-five minutes. The jury were out for one and a half hours before delivering their verdict of guilty but added a recommendation for mercy. The judge asked the foreman to explain the jury's decision. There was no such thing as a majority verdict in 1849. As a result of his query, the jury changed their verdict to guilty of wilful murder.

Observers of the trial stated how Mary had seemed indifferent about the proceedings until now. This changed dramatically when she saw the judge put on his black cap and pronounced sentence of death on her. Now she cried and screamed for mercy as it dawned upon her what was happening. Yet again she professed her innocence, but it was to no avail.

Totally hysterical, she was taken out of the court and returned to the goal.

In the days which followed, Mary reverted to an air of complete indifference to what was happening. She maintained this attitude during visits from her relatives and the chaplain, often behaving badly in the process. The chaplain was so annoyed by Mary's behavior he hit upon a rather drastic scheme to change her attitude.

On 4 August, whilst the governor was elsewhere, Chaplain Reverend

Richard Chapman visited Mary again. On entering the cell, he instructed the matron to fetch him a lighted candle. The matron, Susanna Winter did so and brought it into the cell, but she was horrified to witness what happened next.

Holding the candle in one hand, Chapman took hold of one of Mary's hands and held it over the flame. He enquired if she felt its heat. Initially she ignored him and tried to free her hand, but it was to no avail. Only when she admitted feeling the pain, did he release her. At the same time he warned her such pain was nothing compared to what she would suffer in Hell. After reading some prayers and insisting he had only done it for her own good, the chaplain left.

The matron wasted no time in telling the governor what had happened. He was a humane man and wasted no time in checking up on Mary and was appalled by what he saw. Chapman was suspended and dismissed three days later.

When the governor saw Mary the next day, she confessed to him what had happened.

She had deliberately put the arsenic on the mantlepiece and told her husband it was Epsom salts, hoping for it to be considered nothing more than a tragic accident. When asked why she had done it, Mary replied: 'Why, *my husband was in the habit of going with other women and used me so ill no one knows what I had suffered. But had I known as much as I do now, I would not have done it. For I would rather have left him and went to the workhouse. But I hope God will forgive me.'*

It is impossible to say if this confession was prompted following the candle episode. That afternoon, however, she attended the condemned sermon, where it was reported how her sobbing aloud at times drowned the preacher's voice. In the remaining days prior to her execution, Mary became very penitent and spent much time in prayer. On the actual eve she again confessed her guilt to the new chaplain.

On the following morning, Mary was taken from her cell and five minutes later she was dead.

The notoriety surrounding her case caused a great influx of people into Coventry. It is believed there were between 15,000 and 20,000 witnesses to her execution. An eyewitness stated: '...*was packed so closely with people that you could have walked on their heads and every vantage point was occupied.'*

Mary was buried in the gaol the next day and nobody now knows where her bones lie.

Author's comments

Was Mary a wicked woman?

There is no reason to doubt she had murdered Thomas, albeit with some justification. The motive being to put an end to her unhappy marriage.

The means was by using arsenic which was very easy to obtain. Poisoning is pre-meditated.   Mary's defence of Thomas taking the arsenic by accident might have worked, but only if she had played the part more of a grieving widow instead of a grateful one. She was the author of her own misfortune.

She had ample opportunity to poison Tom and almost certainly did so either in his food or mixing with Epsom salts.

I consider Mary Ball was a wicked woman, albeit not a very clever one. If she had only acted the part of a grieving widow instead of a grateful one, it is unlikely this murder would ever have been discovered. It makes one wonder how many domestic murders remained undiscovered over the centuries.

Undoubtedly, she was also wilful and unconventional. Yet I have some sympathy with her. Mary was in a bad relationship, but in 1849, she had nowhere to turn to for help. Nevertheless, murder is murder and cannot be excused especially when motive, means and opportunity were so clear.

2

Adelaide Blanche Bartlett
née de la Tremouille (1856-?)

Adelaide Blanche Bartlett, née de la Tremouille (pronounced Tremwee) was a real enigma.

Whilst mystery still surrounds her parents, on one matter experts agree: she was an illegitimate child, who was possibly born at Orléans in the Loire Valley, France. One school of thought maintained she came about following a liaison between a well-connected Englishman and a Frenchwoman. There is some suggestion he had been accompanying Queen Victoria on a visit to France, and for propriety's sake, the incident was hushed up. But this is speculation.

She received a French surname, brought up as a Roman Catholic and well provided for by her wealthy family. Her maiden name suggests she took it from her mother's side of the family.

In early 1875, she came to England, to stay with her aunt and uncle, Mr and Mrs William Chamberlain, in Kingston-upon-Thames. Some claim this supports the belief her mother, Clara Chamberlain was definitely English, and her father French.

The Chamberlains were friendly with Charles Bartlett, who brought his brother Edwin, a successful grocer, to meet Adelaide. For Edwin it was love at first sight, but which was not reciprocated.

Nevertheless, a few days later, Adelaide's father had agreed to a wedding, and provided a handsome dowry. His money proved most useful to Edwin's growing grocery business. The couple married in April 1875, but it was a strange relationship from the very outset.

There can be no doubt Edwin was an odd ball.

For instance, he was a **hypochondriac** who knew many of his patent or **quack remedies** contained poisons. Yet he took them to improve his health. On another occasion he had all his teeth sawn off at their roots so he could wear dentures. To say this was a bad idea is an understatement.

Perhaps his most bizarre belief concerned marriage.

Edwin believed a man should have two wives. One for sexual relations and the other for intelligent company and conversation. Following his marriage to Adelaide, Edwin had no intention of going on a honeymoon because he had other plans for his bride. He had earmarked her for companionship and intelligent conversation. Instead of their going away, he sent his new wife off to complete her education elsewhere in England and Belgium.

This was not how Adelaide had expected to be treated as a new bride. Consequently, they did not live together until she returned in 1878. But even then, she was moved into rooms over one of his shops with his brother Frederick. It has been suggested, but never proved conclusively, they became lovers.

Matters changed in 1881 and they finally had sexual intercourse, albeit just once, which resulted in her becoming pregnant. Sadly, it was a difficult birth, but Edwin prevented the midwife from calling in a doctor to assist, because he would not permit any other man to touch his wife. How would he have reacted had he believed Frederick and Adelaide had been lovers? It is difficult to fully understand Edwin's stance on this issue in view of what happened later.

When common sense prevailed and he agreed to call a doctor, it was too late. Adelaide's child was stillborn.

In 1885, the childless couple were living near Wimbledon and Tooting, when they met the Reverend George Dyson, a Wesleyan minister at their local chapel. He was three years younger than Adelaide, and soon became a regular visitor at their house. Edwin explained the idea was for George to improve Adelaide's education on a one-to-one basis and to keep her company whilst he was away on business. George always maintained his visits were to keep the lonely Adelaide company.

It should be said Adelaide was a very attractive woman.

Edwin now seems to have changed his policy regarding other men touching his wife. He encouraged both her and George to be together, and they became lovers. It was thought Edwin became a *voyeur*. He even made it easier for the couple to meet, by paying George's travelling costs to wherever the Bartletts happened to be living.

An unforeseen and most unwanted side effect of Edwin's voyeurism was a reawakening of sexual desire for his wife. Although they were good friends, there had been no physical intimacy, between them for some time. Possibly this was because of the diabolical state of his teeth and gums, which resulted in foul breath or for other reasons.

Edwin probably had **syphilis**, as he was taking **mercury pills**, a well-known treatment for the disease. Whilst there was never any other specific woman identified in Edwin's life, he was clearly having sex elsewhere in accordance with his marital beliefs. It could also have been another reason for his not having sexual relations with Adelaide.

It is easy to imagine how Edwin's renewed sexual interest filled her with horror.

As a rule, neither of them ever visited a doctor, but always relied on their own researches in the event of any medical treatment being needed. She would have made full use of the internet medical pages had she been alive today,

One of Adelaide's researches suggested sprinkling **chloroform** over Edwin's face to stop his sexual advances when he became too amorous. This was the reason she gave later for purchasing it.

On 10 December 1885 Edwin was taken so ill, it was necessary for Dr Alfred Leach to be called. He diagnosed Edwin as suffering from acute **gastritis**, and nervous exhaustion, which was almost certainly caused by overwork, and he prescribed a sedative. The doctor was also concerned about the number of mercury pills Edwin was taking, and which he believed exacerbated the growing problems of the man's gums. In his opinion these were in need of urgent treatment.

In the following days, Edwin was forced to attend a dentist, twice, because of his gums and had twenty-one of his teeth stumps removed. Meanwhile, Dr

Leach's sedative seemed to be working and his health improved. Yet, Edwin insisted Dr Leach arranged for a second opinion, although the doctor did not think was necessary.

Edwin insisted and maintained it was necessary to protect Adelaide from his father. Adelaide and his father disliked one another intensely, and Edwin did not want him to accuse her of poisoning his son.

By Christmas Eve, the second opinion had been carried out by Dr Dudley, who agreed with the earlier diagnosis and the treatment given. As the year ended, with the exception of his teeth, Edwin seemed to have made a good recovery. Edwin's teeth now caused him major problems and Dr Leach arranged to go with him to the dentist.

Dr Leach thought Edwin was suffering from **necrosis**, where the bones in his jaw were starting to die and flake away. If this was so, and the way his gums were receding from the jawbone, made it seem very likely, the disease would result in the complete decaying of his lower jawbone. It was not a pleasant start to the New Year.

On the night of 31st December 1885, Edwin had dined well on jugged hare followed later by oysters, mango relish and chutney. He arranged to have haddock for breakfast. Edwin's illness did not appear to have spoiled his appetite. The household had retired soon after midnight.

But before New Year's Day was very old Edwin Bartlett was dead.

Adelaide's version of events follows.

Having seen Edwin into bed, she then sat alongside him, holding his foot, and fell asleep. Cramp woke her and she realized Edwin was not breathing. Turning him over onto his back, she tried to make him drink some brandy before summoning help. Half an hour later, Dr Leach arrived, and confirmed Edwin was dead. But, finding no obvious reason for his patient's sudden demise, he was unable to issue a death certificate.

An inquest was opened but adjourned.

As Edwin had anticipated, once his father heard of his death, he wasted no time in accusing Adelaide of murder. An **autopsy** was carried out on the following day and samples sent off for analysis. One was found to contain chloroform, which would have led to Edwin's heart muscles ceasing to work. This immediately made Edwin's death suspicious and a police investigation started.

The resumed inquest on 7th February, heard how George had purchased quantities of chloroform for Adelaide: the last being only three days before Edwin's death. It was enough for the police and Adelaide was arrested and charged with Edwin's murder. She was joined later by George Dyson, who was charged with being an accessory to the crime, and the couple were tried at the Old Bailey.

The Crown had a problem from the outset although it used Charles Russell, who became very proficient in prosecuting poisoning cases such as Mary Ann Cotton and Florence Maybrick.

They had only the minimum of evidence against Adelaide, and that was circumstantial. So, they agreed to let George Dyson turn Queen's Evidence and two separate trials were agreed. The Crown then offered no evidence against George, and, as planned, they used him to testify against Adelaide, hoping to boost their flimsy case.

By using George as a prosecution witness, he could now be cross-examined by the defence, which had he still been a defendant, in 1886, would not have been allowed. Adelaide now stood on her own, in the dock, dressed in white, and making a perfect picture of innocence and vulnerability, betrayed by a man she had trusted.

As expected, George testified to having purchased three small bottles of chloroform for Adelaide. He decanted them into a larger bottle and gave it to her before disposing of the bottles. She always denied having used it. Throughout his testimony, apart from kissing Adelaide he denied any other impropriety with her, which may or may not have been true.

One obvious Crown witness was Adelaide's father-in-law, who accused her of having an affair and forging Edwin's will in which she had been left everything.

What the Crown could not show was how Edwin had consumed the chloroform, assuming he had not taken it himself. Suicide was never completely ruled out. It could be argued, he faced a very uncertain future with his dental problems. As no traces, of the chloroform were found in his mouth or anywhere else in his body: only his stomach, it ruled out any suggestions of the drug having been poured in that way. Possibly a tube down his throat might have been used, but the pain of the chloroform in his stomach would have woken him.

Edward Clarke, who defended her, put forward a powerful argument.

How could she, without having any proper medical training or knowledge, have managed to get chloroform into her husband's stomach, without leaving any traces of it in his mouth? In effect, if Adelaide had murdered him, she had done so in such a way that no living surgeon could do. He stressed the way George had deserted her.

The jury was out for just under two hours, which included returning to court to ask for clarification on an issue. It is fair to say they had grave doubts about Adelaide's innocence. Nevertheless, they felt the Crown evidence was insufficient to condemn her.

Adelaide Bartlett was acquitted of the murder of her husband to a round of applause when she was released. Soon afterwards she may have returned to France and possibly lived there with her family. Nevertheless, Adelaide remained a mystery woman to the very end and nobody really knows where she went or what happened to her.

Given the circumstances, doubt must always remain about her acquittal, but according to the letter of the law, it was the right verdict. Edward Clarke always thought Edwin had taken his own life, either deliberately or accidentally, possibly through fear of the necrosis, or because he could not sleep. Others suggest she had hypnotized him into taking the chloroform. Apparently, she was supposed to be credited with having hypnotic powers, although no evidence was produced to support such theories.

Sir James Paget, who was Queen Victoria's surgeon, firmly believed Adelaide had got away with murder. His comments after the trial were: 'She should have told us, in the interests of science, how she did it.'

More than a century on from this case, research has discovered how chloroform, if mixed with brandy, will hang suspended in the alcohol without touching any tissue until arriving in the stomach. Could this have been how the chloroform got into Edwin's stomach. And if so, who put it there? Adelaide, George or Edwin?

Author's comments

Was Adelaide a wicked woman?

This is a difficult question to answer as we know so little about her. The obvious tactic of the Crown was to prove she was a cold calculating person, who had premeditated the murder of her husband. But they were unable to prove it. Certainly, she had motive in getting rid of the weird Edwin. If he was suffering from syphilis and wanted sex with her, that could have been a strong enough motive. And if she was in love with George, the syphilis apart, she needed to dispose of Edwin for their romance to flourish.

The means was obviously by the chloroform, but how had it been administered? There is no doubt it would have blistered Edwin's mouth and throat, if he had drunk it, but no such evidence was found. The cause of his death could be proved, but not how had it been administered. Modern research believes it could have been in brandy, and this is a possible way. We know he was given a brandy. But if Adelaide is to be believed, Edwin was probably already dead when she tried to give it to him. Is her version correct?

From all reports, once the chloroform reached his stomach, Edwin would have been in considerable pain. This being the case, no doubt he would have screamed or at least called out in agony. Yet Adelaide maintained she had heard nothing. Had she used the prescribed sedative to render him unconscious first? There is one report about her neighbours hearing screams. Adelaide maintained they were her's. But were they or did they really come from Edwin?

Assuming she had administered the chloroform in brandy, how had she learnt about that? There had been no other similar murder cases. This was an issue the Crown did not seem to have pursued. Adelaide researched medicines in preference to visiting a doctor. Could this be how she discovered this particular method? And if so, how come nobody else discovered them? We shall never know.

The Crown could not prove the means beyond all reasonable doubt except it was by chloroform.

Being unable to show the means, made it impossible to prove the opportunity, which could only have been shortly before Edwin's death. But how was it done?

Likewise, I do not find wilful an easy question to answer. Adelaide, Edwin and George had a strange *ménage-à-trois* lifestyle where normal standards did not exist. The fact she was an unconventional person did not make her a murderer.

George's role is a strange one.

There can be little doubt he and Adelaide were lovers and Edwin encouraged such an arrangement. Had he not testified against her, there was a strong probability they might have married. His evidence about obtaining the chloroform and disposing of the bottles was damaging to her defence and Adelaide must have felt very betrayed. Had the Crown been able to prove how the chloroform was administered, then his evidence could well have sent her to the gallows. George's evidence was not well received as it highlighted his betrayal of Adelaide. Could it have helped to decide the jury?

This was a scandalous murder trial which made the news with a vengeance. It became the topic of much discussion and speculation over the following days and weeks and still remains unresolved to-day.

Did Adelaide murder Edwin and if so, how did she do it?

But, like Adelaide herself, in the absence of any sudden revelations, this is and always will remain a mystery.

3

Mary Bateman *née* Harker
aka The Yorkshire Witch (1768-1809)

From an early age Mary had criminal tendencies, which resulted in her being dismissed from service whilst a teenager. Not that this punishment changed her ways. On the contrary she continued to steal when and wherever she could. It was too good to last and in 1778 she had fled to Leeds. Fourteen years later she met and quickly married John Bateman, a wheelwright. Despite having four children they had to move regularly because of her continuing criminal activities.

Mary was a proficient confidence trickster who turned whatever she could to her advantage. One such ploy was to look out for serious disasters such as fires and shipwrecks. Having heard about them, Mary quickly went to the scene and made out she was one of the survivors. Suitably dressed in ragged and torn clothing, Mary related how she had lost everything in the disaster and begged for money to feed her children. It was a successful ploy, also used by others, but opportunities such as these happened infrequently, she needed another means of making money.

As the eighteenth century drew to a close, Mary was still in Leeds where she made dresses and told fortunes. Claiming to have supernatural powers, she made money by selling potions which were supposed to cure all manner of illnesses, and especially act against the influence of evil spirits. Many people still believed in witches and other supernatural happenings. It was easy for her to convince them how she possessed supernatural powers which she could use to help them. Her new business enterprise also had a great advantage.

Unlike many crimes, such as theft, it did not carry the death sentence.
The Witchcraft Act 1735 made it a crime to practice as a witch, but at the same time abolished the death penalty, replacing it with a twelve months prison sentence. The last person to hanged for being a witch occurred in 1727.

Nevertheless, Mary had not turned over a new leaf in her dressmaking venture: far from it. In 1803, Mary was believed to have poisoned three people although she was never tried or convicted of doing so.

These first three suspected victims were two Quaker sisters, who lived above their dressmaking shop with their mother. Quite unsuspectingly, they purchased some of Mary's special potions, totally unaware she had sold them poison. Once they had died, Mary wasted no time in robbing their bodies: their shop, living area and anything else she could lay her hands on.
She explained their sudden demise to anyone who asked, how the three had contracted **bubonic plague**, which was a good enough reason to keep them out of the shop. The authorities needed no second urging to keep well away. Consequently, there were no enquiries made or even an inquest.

Having tasted success, Mary continued with her various scams. To help her, she invented a fictitious Mrs Moore who was later supplanted by a Mrs Blythe. She made great play about consulting these women before giving her clients a potion. They would describe their problems to Mary who sent them away for a while to enable her to consult them. On their return, her clients would be given the necessary potion for which they were only too happy to pay.

In 1806, she had a new client in the form of Mrs Rebecca Perigo who was childless. She and her husband, William, were in their mid-40s, not short of money and lived in another part of Leeds. Rebecca's problems involved a fluttering in the breast coupled with the belief she was being haunted by a black dog and other spirits. Her physician, Dr Curzley was unable to help or offer any real advice and left her to survive as best as she could.

Black dogs have long since had a place in English Folklore. They are night-time apparitions usually associated with the Devil or other evil spirits.

With beliefs in black magic superstitions still rife, this diagnosis would have raised few eyebrows.

It set the scene for what happened next.

The Perigos niece visited them at Whitsun and told Rebecca about Mary Bateman who would, hopefully, get rid of the evil spirits. Rebecca was exceedingly grateful, and a meeting was arranged outside, of all places, The Black Dog Inn.

Over the next few months, Mary met regularly with the Perigos. She usually asked for items belonging to Rebecca for sending off to Mrs Blythe, who she explained lived in Scarborough. Neither Perigo had any reason to believe she did not exist. Mary had warned them how the treatment could take at least eighteen months.

Written instructions were received on a regular basis from Mrs Blythe, which Mary insisted were destroyed after having been acted upon. As the weeks progressed, Mrs Blythe made more demands to be given items such as money, silverware, china, tea, sugar, plus a new bed and linen. The excuse was she was having difficulty in sleeping because of the demons she was fighting on Rebecca's behalf.

The money had been sewn into silk purses, and returned to the Perigos, where they were sewn into Rebecca's bedclothes for her to sleep on.

The months passed without any improvement to Rebecca's health. Then a letter from Mrs Blythe warned of an impending illness which might strike one or both of them. This letter instructed them to provide Mary with some honey to be used in making a pudding. She provided some powders for mixing with it. They had to eat these puddings daily for six days. In accordance with the usual instructions, the letter was destroyed.

Also, should any of the puddings not be eaten, they were to be destroyed and not given to anybody else. In the event of them becoming ill, the Perigos were not to consult a doctor.

Neither of them suffered any ill effects from the puddings until the sixth day. Then they suffered from violent stomach cramps and vomiting. They obeyed the instructions about not consulting a doctor, but on 24 May 1807, Rebecca died. William now consulted a doctor who thought she could have been poisoned, but there was no post-mortem carried out and the matter rested.

Meanwhile, William remained seriously ill for some time, although he had long since stopped eating the puddings.

At last he felt well enough to examine some of little silk purses which Mary, via Mrs Blythe, had instructed Rebecca to sew into her bedclothes. When he opened them, William found they contained only copper coins and cabbage leaves and not the more valuable money they had given to Mary.

In total shock, he realized what had happened and decided to do something about it.

He sent a message to Mary asking for some more medicine and arranged to meet her. Mary was delighted because he had provided her with the means of getting rid of an inconvenient witness. She happily met with him and handed over the medicine she had prepared, but her joy was short lived.

As Mary handed over the medicine, she was arrested by the constable William had taken with him. She tried to say William had brought the medicine for her but was not believed as the constable had witnessed everything.

The medicine was found to be a mixture of oatmeal and *arsenic*. When her house was searched, it was found to contain most of the non-perishable valuable articles William and Rebecca had supposedly sent to the fictitious Mrs Blythe. William was shown a sample of Mary's handwriting which he recognized as being identical to Mrs Blythe's.

Mary was committed for trial at the Lent Assizes in York, charged with Rebecca's murder.

As anticipated, she denied the charge.

Damning evidence was produced following an analysis of the remains of the honey pudding. They contained *mercuric chloride*, which is extremely poisonous. Its symptoms closely mirrored those experienced by William and Rebecca.

To be fair, in his summing up, the judge stressed how the jury had to be satisfied poisoning had killed Rebecca, and that Mary had administered it. He added how Mary defrauding the Perigos was not automatic proof of her being guilty of murder. Not that it made any difference. The jury took very little time in finding her guilty.

Before pronouncing sentence of death, the judge asked a now sorrowful Mary if there was any reason why she should not be hanged. In response, she pleaded her belly, which was another way of saying she was pregnant. An examination followed in a locked court, which concluded she was not pregnant, and her sentence of death followed.

Whilst in the condemned cell, she sent her wedding ring to John with the instructions to give it to their daughter. Apparently, she was charging for telling fortunes the night before her execution.

She was hanged the next day at York by William Mutton Curry, the Yorkshire hangman. He had been twice convicted and condemned for sheep stealing and reprieved on both occasions. The last time in 1802, being on condition he remained in prison and acted as hangman when required. He carried out these duties until 1835.

Mary continued denying her criminal activities until Curry opened the trapdoor on the scaffold.

After her execution, Mary's body was sent to Leeds Infirmary for dissection and later put on public display at 3d a time. In this manner, £30 (approximately £1300 today) was raised for the Infirmary. Strips of her skin were tanned and sold off as souvenirs.

Author's comments

Was Mary Bateman wicked?

The answer can only be yes. I cannot find any redeeming features about her case. She set out upon a deliberate deception on William and Rebecca which resulted in murder. This was a carefully planned operation where she took every opportunity to cover her tracks. Destroying the letters was part of her meticulous plan but taking traceable property and keeping it was not so clever. She should have stuck to just money. Granted there was the residue of the poisoned honey to consider, but she could have blamed Mrs Blythe for doing it, with the added advantage of her having vanished.

She obviously panicked when William asked for some more medicine and he needed to be silenced. Her actions here lacked the usual methodical manner in which she operated.

There had been a time lapse since Rebecca's death with no suspicions attached to it. With the benefit of hindsight, she should have given William some harmless medicine on the off chance it could have been a trap. Fortunately, she was worried about him and could not or would not take any more chances.

Despite her plea of not guilty, the Crown had little problems in proving her guilt.

Her motive was robbery. Once both Perigo's were dead, their house would have been stripped bare.

The means was by poison with some residue being found in the honey pudding.

Opportunity might have been a stumbling block, but it could only have come from the honey pudding which Mary had supplied, complete with instructions as to its use. This was backed up by her giving William poison only moments before her arrest.

 Undoubtedly, she was also wilful and unconventional.

One of the other questions to be asked is why, if she was known to be such a thief, did the Leeds inhabitants let her get away with it? The obvious suggestion is they were frightened she really was a witch and would be cursed by her.

Another question concerns the Perigos.

Were they so totally naïve to as believe in Mary and Mrs Blythe? Perhaps William looked upon them as their last hope to cure his wife, especially as the doctor could do nothing for her.

Lastly, where did John Bateman fit into all this?

There does not appear to be any suggestion of his being involved in the murders. Had he been so, his trial and execution would have followed and the couple's children left to the mercy of the parish. I find it difficult to believe he did not know about his wife's thieving habits, but they were a far cry from murder, so I will give him the benefit of the doubt.

Her impatience resulted in a very nasty woman, appropriately known as the Yorkshire Witch, getting her just desserts.

Was Mary Bateman a witch? Only she can answer that question.

4

Elizabeth Berry *née* Finley *aka* Welch

(1856-1887)

Life had not been easy for Elizabeth.

Her first husband was a soldier killed in Afghanistan. She re-married but was a widow again in 1882 when her husband died unexpectedly. Her son died two years later supposedly from sleeping in a damp bed! Her mother, Mary Finley, died in 1885.

Elizabeth became a nurse in Oldham workhouse and earned the annual salary of £25 (approximately £1,850 today). From this she paid £12 to her sister-in-law to care for her daughter Edith Annie Welch, who was eleven years old and lived in Manchester.

It was fair to say Elizabeth was far from having anywhere near enough money. But she would be unable to work if there was no one to care for Edith.

Just after Christmas 1886, Edith and a school friend were invited to spend a few days with Elizabeth at the workhouse. Both children were healthy and happily played together. But, on New Year's Day 1887, Edith was feeling most unwell and was vomiting frequently.

Elizabeth was seen giving her daughter some milky liquid earlier.

Appearing as the concerned mother, Elizabeth took Edith to the workhouse doctor stating how she had eaten something at breakfast which upset her stomach. Dr Paterson gave her some medicine and she recovered slightly. He saw her again the next morning along with a towel containing vomit stains and some blood. Whilst examining this towel, he noticed a strong acidic smell coming from it, and decided to give the child some **bicarbonate** *of soda*, but to do this he needed to borrow the key to the dispensary from Elizabeth.

Whilst he was in there, Dr Patterson noticed the bottle of *medical creosote* was empty and wrote out a prescription for some more which he gave Elizabeth.

Edith's condition worsened, and Dr Patterson found red marks around her mouth. Being concerned, he consulted another doctor, who confirmed his fears that Edith had ingested a corrosive poison. Her condition deteriorated very quickly, and she died soon afterwards. Dr Patterson suspected her death was not accidental and he refused to sign the death certificate. He also asked for a post-mortem to be carried out on Edith's body.

He was not surprised to learn Edith had been poisoned, undoubtedly by medical creosote, which he had inadvertently provided for Elizabeth. Her arrest quickly followed, and she was charged with Edith's murder. Questions were now being asked about the unexpected death of her mother, Mary Finley.

Mary's body was exhumed, and a post-mortem revealed, unsurprisingly, how she too had been poisoned. Elizabeth was further charged with her murder.

More questions were asked about the deaths of her husband and son, but these were not pursued. Perhaps they might have been too long ago, or possibly there was no point. Elizabeth's guilt seemed a forgone conclusion. This became even more apparently when it was discovered how shortly before Edith died, Elizabeth had tried to raise the insurance pay out on her daughter's death. She had tried to disguise it by making the same for her own life for whichever of the two of them died first. She wanted to raise the payout from £10 to £100.

Unbeknown to her at the time of Edith's murder, the insurance company had refused the request.

She was tried at Liverpool Assizes in February 1887, where she pleaded not guilty. Following a four-day trial, she was found guilty and sentenced to hang in Walton Gaol.

It was here where her story took a bizarre twist.

The hangman was James Berry, who although he had the same surname, was not related to her. He was surprised however, to be told by the governor: *'I did not know you were going to hang an old flame, Berry.'*

Apparently, Elizabeth had told the governor about her dancing with James at a policemen's ball in Manchester in 1885. Whilst James obviously knew the name of the convicted prisoner, he had not made the connection. Any doubts he might have had were quickly dispelled once he saw her. It was true, he had danced with her.

There is no suggestion of any sexual involvement between them, and James had been at the ball on his own, as possibly was Elizabeth. It is doubtful if his wife would have approved of their dancing together had she been there. He tried to pretend she was mistaken, but Elizabeth reminded him of the occasion, and they had some more conversation. Elizabeth then had her arms pinioned and she was taken out and hanged. According to the doctor, her death was instantaneous. Before her body was removed, he cut off a lock of her hair as a souvenir.

Clearly, she had made an impression on him.

Author's comments

Was Elizabeth Berry wicked?

I believe there is very little doubt she murdered her mother and daughter, and probably her husband and son. Her motive being money. These deaths came at a time when taking out life insurance plans on people was simple and led to several murders being committed, and not just by women.

The means was by poison, which as a nurse she had access to it, not that it was necessarily obtained in that way. Poisons were easy to obtain from pharmacists. All she had to do was visit one in a place where she was not known and, if asked, give a false address.

When murdering members of your family, who trust you, opportunities appear regularly. In this case when she had specially arranged for Edith to stay with her. Forcing Edith to drink the medical creosote was her big mistake and set alarm bells ringing.

All murders are terrible crimes, but murdering family members, often by painful poisons, is much worse.

I consider Elizabeth Berry to be wicked, wilful and unconventional. There were a few occasions when executioners hanged people they had met previously. The infamous Charlie Peace was one such a person, having previously met his executioner, William Marwood.

5

Annie Besant *née* Wood (1847-1933)

From her earliest days, Irish born Annie held very radical views which did not endear her to the Establishment. To make her even more unpopular, she was a firm supporter of self-rule in Ireland and in India. Annie wrote numerous articles on both topics and was later referred to as Red Annie.

Her father died in 1852 leaving his widow to make a precarious living by running a boarding house for boys who attended Harrow School. It was a full-time task which left her very little time to spend with Annie, who was looked after by a friend in Dorset.

Despite being a devout albeit unconventional Roman Catholic, Annie, then aged nineteen, married an Evangelical minister, Frank Besant, and moved with him to his Lincolnshire parish of Sibsey. It is an understatement to say they regularly quarrelled, usually over the vexed subject of Annie's religion and having her own independence. To make matters worse, she refused to take communion in her husband's church.

It came as no surprise to their friends when they separated in 1874. The mystery was why they had ever married in the first place! Annie became friendly with Charles Bradlaugh, pronounced Bradlow, and soon moved in with him. He too was separated from his spouse.

Bradlaugh was not frightened of controversy.

Working together, they produced a book on birth control in 1877, titled The *Fruits of Philosophy*. Annie was ignorant of the facts of life until her wedding night. Having had two children, she was worried about conceiving another and keen to promote birth control. But, as a body the Church and society in general were outraged at the idea and wanted it stopped. Consequently, the couple were arrested before the book was released.

They appeared in court charged with publishing obscene material. The book was described as *dirty and filthy*, and no one was surprised when they were found guilty and fined £200 each (approx. £12,500 today). This conviction was later quashed, but the publicity did not endear Annie to her husband.

For him it was the last straw. Although Annie made some money from her writing, Frank had always claimed it as his own as he was permitted to do so. This practice was stopped by the **Married Women's Property Act** in 1870. Until then Frank had remained married to ensure he enjoyed the extra income. Now that ceased, he had less need to do so, although a church minister being divorced would be very career damaging: but he had another trick to play.

Following the infamy of the court case, he successfully applied to the courts for custody of their children, accusing Annie of not being a fit and proper person to do so.

The free publicity from this case did Bradlaugh no harm, and in 1880 he was elected as Member of Parliament for Northampton with a comfortable majority. Here he continued being a political activist and on one occasion was forcibly ejected from the House of Commons.

Annie gradually grew away from him and enjoyed using various other lovers when she wanted something. She met her match however, with George Bernard Shaw who rejected her advances. It was her friendship with him which led to Bradlaugh leaving. He neither liked nor approved of Shaw's politics.

In 1881 Annie was elected to the London Board for Tower Hamlets with an overwhelming 15,000 plus votes.

Her notoriety increased in 1887 when she took part in what became known as the Bloody Sunday Demonstration, in and around Trafalgar Square. The gathering was to promote various radical aims including, Home Rule for Ireland, and an end to unemployment. Government reaction was swift and brutal. Police supported by cavalry charged the crowds leading to many casualties and arrests. Annie tried to get herself arrested, but without success. George Bernard Shaw was also there.

During the following year, Annie became very much involved in the Matchmakers' Strike.

In 1888, matches made in England used white phosphorous, which was a deadly substance. If the makers handled it and did not wash their hands before eating, they stood a very good chance of transferring phosphorous to their faces. The result was known as **Phossy Jaw**, which was the common name given to the medical condition of **necrosis** or bone decay. If it was not treated, the victim's face was eaten away, and death inevitably followed.
For most of the women employed in the matchmaking trade, it was little more than slavery.

Matters came to a head following a series of dismissals at the Bryant & May factory. These coincided with the diabolical working conditions in the match making industry being made public and causing a great scandal. The Bryant & May management fought back with a simple rebuttal plan, or so they thought.

They instructed the match girls to write letters in which they would state how well they were treated. Those who refused faced dismissal.

Before electricity was universally installed, naked flames gave light and there was a huge demand for matches, then known as lucifers. They consisted of a small lump of phosphorous on the end of a small stick. Unlike today's safety matches, the phosphorous tips ignited when rubbed against any rough surface. Speed of manufacture was essential because the girls were paid by results and risks were taken. Red phosphorous was much safer, but it was more expensive, so white was more commonly used. Whilst other countries led the way, it would be 1910 before its use was banned in the United Kingdom.

Apart from Phossy Jaw, white phosphorous burnt the skin. Inhaling the fumes could cause heart, liver and kidney failure. The phosphorous impregnated clothes and made the wearers glow. It caused an offensive smell only associated with this trade.

Matchgirls worked a fourteen-hour day standing in poorly ventilated premises for a weekly salary of 4.0s (.20p) (approx. £14 today). From this they had to purchase their own raw materials and monetary fines were imposed for minor misdemeanors. There was no supervision for meals, hence the easy spread of Phossy Jaw. If hygiene rules existed, they were mostly ignored. Any complaints the girls made were filed at foreman level.

No wonder Bryant & May wanted to keep all this quiet.

It is against this background the matchgirls went on strike. Annie took their side where she played a large part. Bryant & May capitulated to stop the adverse publicity, which resulted in being referred to as White Slavery.

After leaving Bradlaugh, Annie converted to socialism thanks to Bernard Shaw and then to Marxism, by William Morris. Following on from the Matchmakers Strike, she became involved in the Dock Strike of 1889.

By 1896 she had become a *clairvoyant* and a keen advocate of *Theosophy*. Moving to India, she agitated there for Home Rule, basing her plans on how she had promoted similar ones for Ireland. The Authorities were not impressed, and she was arrested in 1917, which was the same year Frank died. She received a huge welcome on her release and later visited the United States of America.

During her political career, Annie was a much sought-after speaker, who did not mince her words, or worry about whom she upset. No doubt the Establishment breathed a sigh of relief when she died in 1933.

Author's comments

Whether or not Annie was a wicked woman very much depends on one's viewpoint and place in society. To the government of the day, she was a wicked woman and a regular thorn in their flesh. Yet, she seemed to stay clear of being arrested except over the book and in India. Although she tried to be arrested on Bloody Sunday, it did not happen. Was this because she was protected or had the police been instructed not to do so because of the trouble she would cause? Or to lessen her reputation? There would have been limited custody facilities for dealing with women.

She was wilful as shown by her support of the Matchmakers and Docks strikes. Annie's unconventional behaviour such as living with Bradlaugh and being arrested over the book, raised eyebrows and came at a personal cost. As far as the courts were concerned, she was not a fit and proper person to have the custody of her two children.

Throughout her life Annie was a tireless worker for the underdogs at a time when there was no payment for what she did. How did she survive? Almost certainly by relying on friends. She had been a radical person for most of her life, possibly resenting the fact the Harrow schoolboys had monopolized her mother. We shall never know.

We can be sure she well deserved to be called 'The Champion of Human Freedom'.

6

Mary Blandy (1720-1752) and
William Henry Cranstoun (1714-1752)

Francis Blandy was a successful lawyer and town clerk, living in Henley-on-Thames, Oxfordshire. His only child, Mary, was educated, intelligent and well respected in the area. But, by the time she was twenty-six, there were no immediate prospects of her getting married.

In 1746, Francis, supported by his wife, Anne, considered it was time she did so and as an encouragement to the most suitable man, he offered a dowry of £10,000. (today's value, approximately £1,166,692) …a not inconsiderable sum of money. Surely it would lead to a husband for her! Both parents doted on Mary and were dedicated to ensuring her continued happiness.

In hindsight, this offer was not a very good idea.

As expected, it led to a stream of would be suitors queuing up to make Mary's acquaintance, all of whom she rejected. Then, later in the year, the Honourable Captain William Henry Cranstoun appeared, and it was love at first sight for her.

His father was Lord Cranstoun, a peer of an ancient Scottish family. So was his uncle who had obtained William's commission. Whilst being in Henley on a recruiting drive he met Mary. People described him as 'being short, with freckled pitted skin and clumsy legs.' This is in complete contrast to Mary who is described as 'having a good figure, but her face was pockmarked after smallpox and tended to make her look ordinary.' Clearly, she had some charms which appealed to him, not forgetting the money.

Mary's parents were initially impressed by his background. He came from a noble family and gave the impression of being an ideal husband for their daughter. Do not forget, if Francis was making such a handsome offer of a dowry, what was he worth? And more to the point, how much of his perceived fortune would go to Mary on his death and then to him.

In short, Mary Blandy was a good catch.

Cranstoun had to leave Henley on military business, but on returning wasted no time in resuming his courtship with Mary. The two became lovers and Mary's mother was totally won over by him. It was believed Francis wanted to become grandfather to a lord, which. initially clouded his judgement, but not completely. After all, he was a lawyer and had some doubts about his prospective son-in-law.

Francis let the liaison continue. Nevertheless, he continued to have a niggling doubt about Cranstoun.

And he was proved right.

Versions vary as to how he discovered the man's big secret, but he did so and was horrified at the revelation.

Captain William Henry Cranstoun had a wife and child back up in Scotland.

Francis insisted Mary broke off the romance, but he wasted his breath. The couple continued corresponding with each other. There is a suggestion Mary already knew about Anne Cranstoun née Murray, from whom he received an ample dowry: not that it made any difference to her feelings for him. Cranstoun insisted he had disowned the marriage in 1746, the same year he met Mary and only a few months after his wedding.

Once again versions differ as to why he disowned his marriage, but the author suspects it was because Mary was a far better catch. When Anne's family discovered what was happening, they wrote to Francis Blandy and told him about it.

Francis was adamant there would be no wedding, although Mary pleaded how Cranstoun was trying to get this marriage annulled. One of the reasons given was his wife had strong **Jacobite** loyalties at a time when memories of the abortive '45 Rebellion (1745) were still very fresh. It would certainly not have been in Cranstoun's military career interests to have such a wife.

If anyone thought Anne Cranstoun would give in without a struggle, they were quickly proved wrong.

On 1 March 1748, Anne was granted a decree with an annuity of £40 (approx. £5,000 today) plus £10 (approx. £1,200 today) for her daughter. Cranstoun's argument being they had never been officially married was dismissed.

Meanwhile the lovers continued writing to one another whilst Mary, and her mother, tried to persuade Francis to let the courtship continue. Cranstoun had convinced the women how his marriage was going to be annulled. When Anne Blandy became ill, she insisted Cranstoun was brought back into the house to look after her. He returned and stayed until she died. Mary now had no support in her campaign to make Francis change his mind.

Cranstoun insisted the earlier setback to the marriage annulment was not the end of the matter. There would be an appeal to the House of Lords. But Francis did not believe him and persevered with his opposition.

Cranstoun now decided a more drastic approach was needed.

When he stayed with the Blandys after Anne's death, he became aware of the supernatural beliefs harboured in the house. He added to them with tales of phantom music, footsteps and dress rustlings, but they were all untrue. At the same time, Mary told the neighbours how she had heard music in the house, which was believed to be a sure sign of an impending death within the next twelve months. Was she setting the scene for her father's death?

After being banned from the house, Cranstoun returned to Scotland, and sent some Scottish jewellery to Mary which consisted of semi-hard stones in settings which were currently very popular. He enclosed a covering letter which referred to earlier conversations and a package containing some powders. The letter explained it was to clean the pebbles, but her real instructions were to mix them it her father's tea.

Mary was told they were love powders aimed at making her father less anti his prospective son-in-law. He described them as '*Powders to clean the Scotch pebbles,*' suggesting such a description should allay any suspicions.

The powders duly arrived in 1751 and Mary gave them to her father.

Undoubtedly, they were ***arsenic*** and caused him a considerable amount of pain and suffering. Today, such symptoms of severe intestinal pains coupled with losing some teeth would be very indicative of arsenic poisoning, which was not so evident in the eighteenth century.

Tooth decay was rampant in 1751, with sugar being widely available from the West Indies, for those who could afford it. Francis was taken ill after drinking some of the poisoned tea, but later recovered.

Soon afterwards he did not drink his breakfast tea, which was given to Ann Emmet, a charwoman, who became seriously ill after drinking it. Mary sent her broth and wine to speed her recovery. Was this a genuine offer of help or a guilty conscience? One of the servants had also been taken ill after drinking the same tea.

More powders came and this time, following Cranstoun's recommendations, Mary put them in her father's gruel where they mixed more easily.

Arsenic dissolves in something hot but creates a residue when cooled. Gruel was a popular albeit thinner version of porridge which could be eaten or drunk. In the early part of August 1751, Francis was taken ill again and so was Ann Emmet following their consuming some gruel from the same pot.

The Blandy household was concerned, and maid Susannah Gunnell suspected what was happening, So she took the pot of gruel and her suspicions to a neighbour, Mrs Mounteney, who summoned the apothecary Mr Norton. He had regularly attended the Blandy family for years and took the gruel for analysis. It was found to contain arsenic. But Susannah was not finished and spoke to Francis the next day and told him she thought he was being poisoned by his daughter.

When asked where Mary had obtained the poison, she blamed Cranstoun and Francis agreed with her. He saw Mary soon afterwards and accused her of poisoning him. Turning away from her, he left the kitchen and Mary knew she had to act fast.

Mary went straight up to her bedroom, where she gathered all the letters from Cranstoun and threw them and the remaining packet of powder onto the fire. Just then Mary was distracted by a maid putting more logs on the fire and she left the room. The maid was unable to rescue the letters but succeeded with the powder.

This too was found to be arsenic.

As the day progressed, Francis deteriorated, and Mary agreed for Dr Anthony Addington from nearby Reading to be called. He was highly recommended, and the ensuing court case would ensure his rightful place in the science of forensic chemistry in criminal investigations.

It was obvious Francis was dying, and Mary had been confined in her room, effectively under arrest with guards posted outside the door.

What happened next is open to interpretation.

At one stage the local sexton, who was one several local men who had been interested in the offer of £10,000 to marry Mary, was her guard. He left his post to go and dig a grave, believed to be for Francis. Whilst he was gone, Mary slipped out of the house having supposedly bribed some of the staff to acquire a carriage for her.

She did not get very far. Only being partly dressed and with numerous people watching the house, she was soon caught.

At her trial, Mary was adamant she was not running away, but just needed to get out of the house and had not stopped to dress. Many believed her, but if she had been that innocent, why the bribes for a carriage?

Mary appeared at Oxford Assizes on 3 March 1752 charged with her father's murder.

She entered a plea of not guilty and continued maintaining her belief the powder was not arsenic, but a love *philtre* for Francis. The jury were not impressed and found her guilty after a thirteen hours trial, in which Dr Addington made a name for himself as a Crown witness. They had not bothered to retire, so certain were they of their verdict.

This was the first-time medical evidence had been presented in a criminal trial. Addington convinced the jury how arsenic had been given to Francis which had ultimately caused his death. By today's standards, it was very primitive, but nevertheless it was a start. Forensic science had arrived and would continue to grow as it still does today.

Sentence of death followed, and her execution was scheduled for 6 April. Although ceaselessly denying the charge, she is best remembered for complaining about the height of the gallows… *'For the sake of decency, gentlemen, don't hang me so high.'*

Surprisingly her body was taken back to Henley-on-Thames and buried between her parents, which seems a strange thing to do, given the circumstances of his death. It was not a regular practice to bury murderers alongside their victims, family or otherwise.

Meanwhile, what had happened to Cranstoun who is the real villain of the piece?

Having heard about Mary's arrest, he quickly fled from Scotland to France. It was sufficient for him to do as little as that. Extradition did not arrive until 1870, so he had nothing to worry about. He died in December the same year of an unknown cause which was recorded as natural causes.

Almost certainly it was a combination of cardiac and kidney failure Such money he had was left to his abandoned wife and daughter.

His death should have laid the whole affair to rest which it did, at least initially, apart from the odd sightings of Mary's ghost in and around Henley.

The story was resurrected in 1969.

A play, titled *The Hanging Wood* had been written about the Mary Blandy case, and was arranged to be performed at the Kenton Theatre in Henley-on-Thames. From the very outset, the production was plagued by all manner of problems.

Lights would be switched on and off and a mirror fell and shattered on the floor. These events mainly happened when Mary's name was mentioned. Once a strange, almost ghostly looking woman, who was not a member of the cast, was seen. She did not worry the cast, as ghosts in theatres are considered lucky. She has appeared again when *The Hanging Wood* was being performed. Was she Mary's ghost?

But even this haunting is not really the end of the affair.

The whole murder undoubtedly centred around Francis Blandy's offer of a £10,000 to whoever married his daughter. It was an incredible sum of money which clearly tempted Cranstoun. He also believed Francis Blandy had much more in addition to this dowry. Even without this belief, it still made Mary a good catch and would set him up nicely, after getting rid of his existing wife.

The real irony is Francis Blandy did not have £10,000 to give as a dowry. It is believed his total assets were £4,000 (approximately £466,676 today). It was still a hefty sum, which if he had been a skilled tradesman was the equivalent of 40,000 days wages.

Author's comments

Was Mary Blandy innocent, being blinded by love?

If yes, why did she try to burn the remaining arsenic and letters from Cranstoun, once she knew the game was up? Not really the actions of an innocent person. Likewise, how innocent was her abortive flight? Granted, she was not properly dressed, but she had arranged for a carriage to be waiting for her. Are these the actions of genuine innocent person?

Was she truly innocent when reading Cranstoun's cryptic comments in his letters about disguising the powder?

Their motive for murdering Francis clearly was to get him out of the way. He was the impediment to their marriage and ultimately Cranstoun's wealth or so he believed.

The means was via Francis's tea and later gruel which Mary prepared complete with the arsenic. She had plenty of opportunities to give it to her father. It can be argued this was murder by proxy, but she was fully implicated in it. If she was unaware it was arsenic, how could she explain the servant being taken ill? And, the servants did not trust her. Why? If they suspected something was seriously wrong, so should an intelligent and well-educated young woman.

I think Mary Blandy was wicked and very wilful. Having been banned from seeing and communicating with Cranstoun, she disobeyed her father and carried on doing so. Unlike some of the other characters in this book, Mary's claim to being unconventional only involves her dealings with Cranstoun.

Whilst the evidence points to it being Cranstoun's idea to give her father the philtre, she clearly went along with it. At some stage she would have realized what was happening, yet her love or more probably infatuation with him, insisted she carry on. Thus, she became the willing instrument in a murder by proxy. I wonder if Cranstoun had been around locally, whether he would have done the poisoning himself, or persuaded Mary to do it? I suspect he would have had her do it, so if anything went wrong, she would be nicely set up to take the blame. He was only interested in himself and fled to escape justice.

Yet he did not outlive Mary for very long. He forgot that whilst the mills of justice may grind slowly, they grind exceedingly fine.

7

Elizabeth Brandish (?-1897/8-?)

On 8 September 1897, Mr and Mrs Posts at Wye, in Kent, were devastated. A woman whom they only knew as Mrs Edwards, had come back into their lives and reclaimed her young son. She said they were going back to live at Ettington, in Warwickshire.

The Posts had been caring for Rees Thomas Yells Brandish, which was his real name, since 1895, for £1 (approximately £56 today) per month, and the payments were always made regularly by his mother. Over the months they had looked upon him as their own child, whilst their niece, Sarah Urben did most of the work of bringing Rees up. It had been a happy arrangement, but their pleas to keep the boy were ignored. During her short stay with the Posts, Mrs Edwards acquired a large tin box complete with two padlocks.

Two days later, the Posts and Sarah bade a tearful farewell to Rees. They were permitted, however, to keep a lock of his hair.

By the time Mrs Edwards, or to use her real name Elizabeth Brandish, arrived in Ettington, she still had her tin box, but no child.

A boy had been seen with her at Towcester but he was not on the train when it arrived st Ettington.

On arriving at the railway station, she was very fretful about her tin box and would not be separated from it. As there no carriers available, she carried it most of the way herself. Elizabeth's destination was her brother George's Drybank Farm in Ettington, where he lived with his wife, Louisa. She was the only person who knew her sister-in-law's guilty secret.

Elizabeth had given birth to an illegitimate child whilst employed as a nurse in Kent. Louisa knew the child had been adopted. It is a matter of conjecture if she knew the full circumstances of the arrangement with the Posts. Certainly, she was not surprised when Elizabeth arrived without the boy.

After staying just two days, Elizabeth said she was moving to Clent, near Bromsgrove in Worcestershire, to start a new job. In fact, that was not the case. She had recently nursed the dying wife of Police Sergeant Roger Hill Narramore of the Worcestershire County Constabulary, who had **pneumonia**. Since her death, she and Roger had become close and there was a possibility of marriage in the foreseeable future.

When Elizabeth left the Posts, she talked about going back to live in Ettington. She wrote to them as promised, but the descriptions of young Rees, did not seem to refer to him. Sarah was concerned and wrote to the Ettington vicar, asking him to make sure Mrs Edwards and young Rees were well.

The vicar was unsure what to do when he received the letter. He did not know of any woman and a young boy recently arriving in the village, but nevertheless he visited Drybank Farm. Louisa confirmed Elizabeth had come alone so he replied as such to Sarah. Now very concerned, she called in the police.

As nobody in Ettington matched these very vague descriptions, the enquiry went back to the Kent police. From there the trail ultimately led back to Drybank Farm and thence on to Clent, where Elizabeth was interviewed by Police Sergeant Pugh.

She admitted being Mrs Edwards who had fostered her illegitimate nine-week old son with the Posts. Elizabeth further admitted taking the boy back from them and giving him to a woman on the same train where they had arranged to meet. Apparently, she had met this woman the previous year. Maintaining she was desperate for a child, Elizabeth agreed to let her have Rees. She had never asked for the mystery woman's name and address.

Meanwhile, the police under the command of Inspector James Ravenhall of the Warwickshire Constabulary, were searching Drybank Farm, but had found nothing. Then a sharp-eyed officer spotted what appeared to be **quicklime**, which had only been spread around a few plants. This did not seem right to him. He expected it to have been spread around all the plants:

not just a few of them.

The vegetable patch was dug up and the decomposing remains of a small boy, aged about two to two-and-a-half years old was discovered.

As he had been buried in quicklime, any facial identification was impossible. The only clues were a dental pattern which matched a tooth the Posts had and a similar matching lock of hair. There was no DNA in 1897 and very limited forensic knowledge compared with today. Nevertheless, the legal authorities considered there was enough evidence to identify him as the missing Rees.

Elizabeth's arrest quickly followed, and she was charged with the boy's murder.

Her trial began in March 1898 at Warwick Assizes and was most sensational.

Whilst it might have seemed an open and shut case, nothing was further from the truth.

The very first problems began before the trial started. This case had aroused such a morbid interest, it resulted in an unprecedented number of would-be spectators wanting access to the public gallery, to witness the proceedings. Consequently, admission had to be by tickets, which meant approximately ninety percent of all the applicants were unable to get into the court building, let alone view the proceedings. Such restrictions on people attending notorious trials were not unknown. Admittance by ticket was obviously not popular, but no one had a better idea.

As anticipated, Elizabeth pleaded not guilty and many witnesses were called.

The biggest problem facing the Crown was the identification of the body found at Drybank Farm. Elizabeth stuck rigidly to her tale of having given Rees away to a woman on the train. Railway staff at Bletchley confirmed having seen her with a child, but who was dressed in different clothes to the ones Rees had been wearing when he left the Posts. Was it the same child? Or were the staff mistaken. She changed trains at Towcester and upgraded to a second-class compartment which she had to herself. There was no mention of a child being with her.

Her brother George agreed there was so much quicklime around his farm, it was impossible to tell if any was missing. He also agreed it was possible for anyone to leave the farm during the night without any problems. It was the quicklime which was the biggest problem for the Crown.

It had rendered a proper inspection of the body impossible, along with any facial recognition. All the experts could say about the hair on the body and the lock which the Posts had kept was that it was similar. Likewise, the fact the body had similar teeth missing to those described by the Posts was not conclusive evidence.

In brief, no one could be certain the body belonged to Rees. And to add to the Crown's problems, it could not be proved how the boy had died.

Finding a motive was easier. Elizabeth and Roger Narramore were clearly much attracted to one another, and his daughters liked her. To all appearances it seemed to be a perfect match. But this was the nineteenth century and police officers were not permitted to marry without the consent of the chief constable. He would only give it after the prospective bride and her family's background had been fully investigated, and here was the problem.

There was a possibility, albeit remote, details of her illegitimate son would be discovered. Once that happened, Sergeant Narramore would be given two choices. He could marry Elizabeth or stay in the police: but not do both.

The Crown concentrated on this being her motive for murdering Rees.

The jury deliberated the case for just over three hours before informing the judge they were unable to reach a verdict. He accepted their decision, but ordered a re-trial, albeit not at the current Assizes. They were also excused jury service for the next five years. It transpired later how there was just one dissenting juror, whose views might have been biased as he was against capital punishment. He later gave an interview to the press.

Elizabeth's Defence team used the interim time well and were able to plug some of the gaps exposed in the first trial.

Admission to the second trial was just as chaotic as it had been for the first one.

Once everyone was settled, the judge, Mr Justice Darling harangued the media for the interview they had published with the dissenting juror. Elizabeth had now been in custody for nine months, which might possibly have resulted in some sympathy for her.

The Crown's evidence had not really changed since the previous trial, except in the case of Roger Narramore. He was now described as a former police sergeant from Clent. It was unclear whether he had been posted elsewhere or left the Constabulary. The author suspects it was probably the latter, as being closely associated with a murder suspect would have seriously damaged his career. Either way, remaining at Clent would not have been an option.

It came as no surprise to the Crown how the outcome of the trial depended on the identification of the body. If the boy could not be positively identified as being Rees Brandish, the chances of her being found guilty were incredibly slim. Without such evidence, the body's link to Elizabeth could not be proved. There was a further difficulty about the cause of his death. The medical experts thought he might have been strangled, yet it was known he had **whooping cough** when Elizabeth collected him.

His death from natural causes could not be ruled out.

Another problem involved the witness at Bletchley. He was adamant the child he saw was Rees who had been dressed in different clothes to the ones he was wearing when he had left the Posts. Was it likely, argued the defence, that Elizabeth would buy the boy some new clothes shortly before killing him? This was important because she had not taken any spare clothes with him from Kent.

Her defence had always been she had not killed Rees but given him away.

With no hard evidence the body belonged to Rees or what had killed him, there was only one verdict the jury could deliver...Not Guilty.

It was not a popular verdict, but in fairness to the jury, what other one could they have delivered? Had it been in Scotland, there was the third option of *Not Proven*. Possibly, if it had not been for the dissenting juror, a guilty verdict might have been delivered at the first trial.

Whatever happened, young Rees disappeared and was never seen again.

Whilst such an ignominious end to any young child's short life was an outrage, however it happened, there was still a disgraceful and shameful epilogue to come. After having endured a secret disposal in a cabbage patch, it might have possibly made some amends for there to be a proper burial service for him.

But no!

Back in Ettington, the vicar was absent. The Methodist preacher was approached, but he insisted on being given forty-eight hours-notice. But even then, he did not think a church service would be permitted. His argument being there was no evidence of the dead child ever having been baptized.

In the end, the unidentified boy was buried in an unmarked grave with no service. Only the undertaker's wife and two women were there. No members of the Brandish family attended.

Apparently, none of the letters Elizabeth sent to Roger Narramore when she was in prison, were ever answered.

Author's comments

It is a fundamental principle of English Law that the Crown must prove its case beyond reasonable doubt. They must prove guilt: the defence does not have to prove their innocence. This case depended almost entirely on **circumstantial evidence**, which contained doubts, principally about identification of the body and cause of his death. Consequently, rightly or wrongly, the jury gave the correct verdict based solely on the available evidence. Today it would have been different and DNA would have made or broken the case.

I am certain the body in the cabbage patch was that of little Rees, and I believe Elizabeth put him there. But it was all circumstantial evidence. Undoubtedly the tin box was purchased to hide his body and to carry it around. She had it with her on arrival at Ettington and would not let anyone else handle it. Today's forensic skills would have found traces of Rees or any other body having been inside it.

If we believe her story about giving Rees away in the train, why when given the tremendous amount of publicity, did this mystery woman not come forward? Or did she have her own guilty secret? Then, there is the Bletchley witness. Did he see Rees albeit wearing different clothes? The defence had a valid argument when asking why should she provide Rees with new clothes shortly before killing him? Was it a deliberate move to fool potential witnesses? I believe it could have been. After all, she had gone to the trouble of obtaining the tin box, this was a pre-meditated well-planned crime and not one committed on the spur of the moment.

The motive would have been to remove any bar to her marriage to Sergeant Narramore. But there was no evidence of means and only a vague opportunity whilst on the train. Why did she find it necessary to kill Rees if she did? He was safely and happily well away in Kent, but I suppose she was worried about the ever-present possibility he might suddenly surface and so the poor boy had to go.

Is it possible he might have died from natural causes on the train and she panicked? Hence her concealing his body so as not to interfere with her marriage plans. Maybe, but there is still the mystery of the tin trunk and why did she have it?

It could have been so much different if only poor Rees had been positively identified.

The way Rees was treated when it came to his burial is appalling. Perhaps we can excuse the absent vicar, but for the other one to doubt he could be buried in hallowed ground because his baptism could not be proved is inexcusable.

This case is rightly sometimes referred to as *The Ettington Sensation*.

Interestingly, in 1902 there was a murder in North Warwickshire, where a mother, her daughter and ten days old baby were murdered. There was no problem with the baby being buried with his mother. It seems the question about baptism in this instance was never an issue.

Irrespective of the court's findings, I have no hesitation in calling Elizabeth Brandish a wicked and wilful woman. She was an unconventional mother in the way she treated her son regardless of whether she caused his death or not.

8

Florence Bravo *née* Campbell *aka Ricardo*
(1845-1878)

If he had realized how this new patient would dramatically change his life, Dr James Manby Gully would never have taken her on, when she appeared in 1870. He was introduced to her as Mrs Florence Ricardo. He had treated her once as a child, but now she had developed into a very attractive woman.

Gully first arrived in Malvern, Worcestershire, during 1842 where he set up a new **hydrotherapy** clinic. Here he treated patients using Malvern water and it soon became very successful. Well ahead of his time in many ways, he was concerned about the quantity of drugs being taken by patients and wanted to use alternative remedies. His treatment involved drinking Malvern water and being wrapped in wet sheets. He already had a very good reputation in this field when Florence appeared.

On the domestic front, his first wife had died and his second was a very domineering woman. They parted company after just five years of marriage.

Florence was unhappily married to Captain Alexander Ricardo, formerly of the Grenadier Guards, who had been pressurized by her to resign his commission. The idea being for them to concentrate on having a family, with him being at home, and not away on campaign somewhere. It proved to be a bad idea because Ricardo clearly was not impressed by this new arrangement. In retaliation, he embarked on a series of affairs and later became violent towards her.

Florence left him and returned to her parents, Robert Tertius and

Ann Campbell, wanting a divorce. Instead of getting the help she needed, Florence met a problem. Thanks to their high standing in society, they could not possibly contemplate such an idea. As a gesture, however, instead of returning her to Ricardo immediately, they took her to see their old friend, Dr Gully, trusting him to sort out her problems.

He did so, but not in the way they had envisaged.

Gully wasted no time in persuading her to divorce Ricardo and offered to make all the arrangements. In a very short time, Florence had become Gully's mistress. Matters were greatly helped in 1871 when Ricardo died.

Their affair intensified, becoming sexual during a trip to Bavaria. The servants quickly realized what was happening, but either said nothing or were bribed to keep quiet. Remember, Florence was only in her twenties whilst he was in his sixties.

Several weeks later, Florence persuaded him to give up his practice in Malvern and move with her to a more exciting part of the world: London. Florence purchased a house known as *The Priory*. For propriety's sake, not that it made a great difference, they had different houses albeit not too far apart from each other.

Meanwhile, Florence had taken in Jane Cannon Cox as a companion, who became increasingly involved in her life and had her own plans for Florence.

Cox obviously knew about Florence and Gully and was content to wait for the ideal moment to change things. When the time was ripe, she would work on Florence to break off her relationship with him. Whilst it might be acceptable for the servants to know about the affair, it was a different matter where friends and family were concerned. It could never remain a secret. Finally the scandal inevitably broke and put them under a great deal of pressure.

But worse was to come.

In early 1873, Florence had a fresh problem: she was pregnant, and Gully was obviously the father. Whilst she could cope with the scandal of having a lover, an illegitimate child would finish her in society. There was only one possible answer.

Gully aborted her pregnancy.

Officially he operated on her to remove a tumour. To ensure this was the only story to be circulated, Cox was his sole assistant during the operation. Gully was taking a great risk in more ways than one as abortions were illegal. Although the offence no longer carried the death penalty, a prison sentence would follow with other ramifications on his being able to practice as a doctor.

When it was over, the abortion put paid to any further sexual relations between them. Even if they might possibly remain friends, the two of them could never be lovers again. This was the moment Cox had waited for to put her plans into operation.

She persuaded Florence to break off all further communications with Gully, which she ultimately did.

There can be little doubt Cox was a matchmaker and she engineered the initial meeting between Florence and barrister Charles Delauney Turner Bravo. He wasted no time in asking Florence to marry him and she accepted. Throughout their courtship, she regularly met up with Gully and confided in him about her forthcoming marriage.

Any thoughts he may have entertained about her coming back to him, were quashed when she married Bravo in December 1875. Gully felt bitter and betrayed. He had sacrificed his career and social standing for her, only to be cast aside in favour of a much younger man. Initially he considered selling up in London and returning to Europe, but later changed his mind.

Having decided to stay in London, he instructed his servants that Florence was never to be admitted into his house under any pretext. If Gully thought he would never be involved with her again, he was sadly mistaken.

Charles Bravo knew about Gully's affair with Florence and was far from pleased to find her former lover was not now going abroad but remaining in London.

It was about now when the Bravos first received anonymous abusive letters. Whilst the identity of their writer has never been discovered, Gully remains the number one suspect.

Florence's marriage to Bravo was both short and unpleasant.

Thanks to the **Married Women's Property Act 1870**, she owned *The Priory* and kept her own money. Nevertheless, it did not take Bravo long to assume control of it and start re-arranging her staff. Suddenly she was no longer in control: but he was.

He was soon making other demands.

In addition to opening all her mail, he was making constant sexual demands. With memories of her recent abortion still fresh in her mind, Florence could not cope with them. In many respects it was a re-run of her earlier marriage to Alexander Ricardo, but with an extra barb.

Bravo never missed any opportunity to remind his wife of her affair with Gully. This had always rankled ever since she told him, and he never intended to let her forget it. And to make matters worse, Gully did not live too far away.

Finally, she could bear it no longer and went back to her parents, which might not have been the best idea. With Florence safely out of the way, it enabled Bravo to strengthen his hold on *The Priory*. One of his first changes was to dismiss Cox and in doing so, made himself a very dangerous enemy. At the same time, he begged Florence to come home.

Whilst this idea did not appeal to her, Florence was now two months pregnant and she was worried about Cox. When Florence thought about it, she knew there was no real choice and returned to *The Priory*.

Florence miscarried soon after her return, not that it made any difference to Bravo and his sexual demands. She quickly re-employed Cox who then moved into her bedroom, effectively banning Bravo from it.

Following on from the miscarriage, Florence became very debilitated, which worried Cox.

For some time, she had been seeing Gully having met him once quite by chance. Despite their embarrassment of not having parted previously on the best of terms, they met more regularly. On their latest occasion, she told him about the miscarriage and asked if he could prescribe something to help Florence sleep.

Three days later a bottle labelled poison was delivered to her house in Notting Hill. She had been expecting some **Laurel water** and this package surprised her, so she did not pass it on to Florence. There was never any suggestion it had been sent by Gully. Its sender remains unknown.

In less than a month after her miscarriage, Bravo was back in his wife's bed, desperate to have a son. It did not take him long to get her pregnant again, but a further miscarriage soon followed. Soon afterwards, Bravo first started feeling unwell although it only lasted for a few hours. His next bout of illness on 18th April would have a fatal result.

Bravo had been out riding, but he was in a badly shaken state on his return, claiming his horse had bolted. After a leisurely bath, he joined Florence and Cox for dinner, during which he received a letter commenting on his gambling debts which infuriated him.

He remained upset for the remainder of the meal.

His temper worsened when he heard Florence ordering a servant to put some wine in her bedroom for a nightcap. He accused her of drinking too much and stormed off to bed. Albeit unwillingly, he was sleeping on his own because Florence pleaded, she was not yet over her latest miscarriage.

Suddenly he called out for hot water.

A maid, Mary Ann Keeber, went to see what was wrong and found him hot, sweaty and shrieking for hot water. Moments later, he had opened the window and vomited over the lower roof.

Mary Ann went to seek help.

Cox quickly went with her to the bedroom. Having taken one look at Bravo, she ordered Mary Ann to fetch some mustard mixed in coffee to make him sick, and hopefully bring up whatever was causing the problem. It worked and he vomited again, but this time into a basin which Cox instructed to be cleaned immediately. Then she sent for Florence's personal doctor although he lived some distance away.

Florence was now awake and appeared in the bedroom, where she decided not to wait for Dr Harrison to arrive but sent for a closer one. Both doctors examined the now unconscious Bravo and came to the same conclusion.

He had been poisoned but they had no idea what had been used.

Two more doctors arrived, Royes Bell who was Bravo's cousin and George Johnson. Bravo was now conscious, and they were able to ask him what he had taken. He replied just **laudanum** for toothache. The doctors were not convinced because his symptoms were wrong for such an overdose.

Cox now told them what Bravo had just said to her, which they had apparently not heard: '*I've taken some of that poison: don't tell Florence.*' He did not elaborate on what he had taken. For the remaining hours of his life, he continually insisted it was only laudanum he had taken. Another specimen of his vomit was examined but revealed nothing.

Considerable doubt exists about what, if anything, he said to Jane Cox.

According to the evidence, she was the only person to have heard these words. The doctors denied having heard anything. James Ruddick, author of *Death at the Priory*, later carried out tests in Bravo's bedroom. Regardless of how quietly he spoke, he could always be heard. If he could be heard, why were the doctors unable to do so? Interestingly, Mary Ann did not hear the confession and she was closer to Bravo than the doctors.

This was a very important piece of evidence which the police did not check out. Were they completely overawed by the social standing of the people they were interviewing, or was it just shoddy police work?

And why did Cox lie about this confession as she must have done? Was it to protect Florence who she knew or suspected might have poisoned Charles Bravo? Or had she done it herself in revenge for having been dismissed earlier and the way he continually treated Florence? If she poisoned him, this was one way to shift the blame from herself onto him.

Sir William Gull, Queen Victoria's own doctor also attended when summoned by Florence. He examined Bravo and came straight to the point. The man was dying, and he needed to tell them what had happened. If he did not do so, Sir William added, there was a very real risk of somebody being wrongly blamed for poisoning him. Bravo kept to the same story of only taking laudanum.

He died in the early hours of Friday 21st April 1876.

The subsequent post-mortem showed his death as being the result of '*swallowing a large dose of **tartar emetic***' which is a derivative of ***antimony***.

The pathologist stated if someone was going to commit suicide by taking poison, antimony, was the last one they would use. It was rated as being one of the most painful chemicals available.

The police enquiry into his death was regularly obstructed.

In 1876, professional policing was still in its infancy and detection mainly concentrated around crimes against property and assaults. Murder investigators lacked experience, especially when investigating the upper classes. To be fair, in this case there were no eyewitnesses and any prosecution would have to rely on circumstantial evidence, which is never ideal. Likewise, the upper classes resented being questioned by the police, let alone even acknowledging their existence. Florence's father was a typical example.

He was wealthy, a justice of the peace and former high sheriff. In his opinion Bravo had committed suicide and that was the end of the matter. His comments were to the effect that was the verdict he would get within five minutes at the inquest.

Thanks to his influence what can best be described as a closed or even secret inquest was held at *The Priory*. The coroner excluded the press and saw no reason to disagree with Robert Campbell's suggestion of suicide. The verdict was not quite as Robert Campbell had envisaged and it stated Bravo *'had been poisoned'* but could not confirm how the poison was administered.

Whilst it might have satisfied Robert, it was nowhere near the end of the matter.

Joseph Bravo, Charles's father was far from satisfied and referred the matter to Scotland Yard and a full-scale enquiry began. A second inquest took place a few weeks later which lasted for twenty-three days. So much for Robert wanting a quiet and private affair. This was what he had dreaded.

Much of the inquest centred around the salacious details of Florence's affair with Gully and ruined them and others in the process. One newspaper called her: '...*a miserable woman who indulged in a disgraceful connection.*' Another wrote: '*She was a miserable adulteress and an inebriate, selfish and self-willed, a bad daughter and a worse wife.*'

The jury basically overturned the first verdict and agreed Bravo had been wilfully murdered by person or persons unknown. This verdict has never been altered and no one has ever been charged with his death.

Dr Gully was heavily criticized in the press, for having an affair with a woman who was young enough to be his granddaughter. He was ostracized by his own daughter and moved in with his widowed sisters. Irrespective of his previous good works and important patients, he never recovered his reputation and died in 1883.

Robert Campbell became ill and his family business went bankrupt, possibly as a result of his daughter's scandal. He was forced to sell all his property at home and abroad to pay off his debts.

Florence was also ruined. Her brother William, the only one of her siblings who still spoke to her, suggested she moved to Australia with him, but she declined. Instead, she moved to Southsea and drank herself to death in 1878, aged just thirty-three years old.

Author's comments

Florence is a complicated character. If she had nothing to do with Bravo's death, was she a wicked woman?

In the eyes of Victorian society, her affair with Gully made her so, although it is not clear who first seduced who. In any event she suffered for it once it became not just known, but also hit the press. What more could they want? A suspicious death, an attractive woman and a sex scandal. But does this make her wicked?

Was Bravo murdered and this is by no means clear, as his death could have been suicide or an accident? Assuming it was murder, then Florence is one of the main suspects.

Being in yet another abusive relationship aggravated by Bravo continually wanting sexual intercourse, her motive could quite simply have been to put an end to it. She knew there would be little or no help from her parents, especially with their preoccupation with social standing in society. They had not really helped with her marriage to Alexander Ricardo.

The means quite clearly was the tartar emetic. When this was disclosed, Robert Campbell maintained he had never heard of it. He was told just about every stable in the country would have it on their premises. Thus, the means were easily available, not only to Florence but also to all other members of staff.

Knowing her husband's eating and drinking habits, the opportunity would not have been difficult for anyone to have poisoned him, not just Florence.

There were other suspects:

A. Jane Cox was responsible for introducing Florence to Bravo who later wanted her dismissed permanently. This caused her a few problems, but she was soon due to inherit a considerable amount of money, so finance should not have been a problem. And there were her secret meetings with Gully. Had she decided to murder Bravo for Florence's sake? Was that her motive? It was suggested her cleaning his vomit from the roof and basin destroyed valuable evidence. But subsequent examination of other similar specimens did not reveal any tartar emetic. Interestingly no doctor recalled her telling them about Bravo commenting on taking poison. The inference being that this is a false statement with the obvious intention of protecting Florence or herself!

The means and opportunity remain the same.

B. George Griffiths was the coachman dismissed by Bravo. He would have known about tartar emetic and had a good motive of wanting revenge, but when did he have the opportunity? He had once been Gully's coachman and then for Florence where he was dismissed in 1872. But he was re-employed there in 1875.

C. Dr James Manby Gully had a good motive to get rid of Bravo for Florence's sake. He knew what was happening thanks to Jane Cox and could have supplied her with the poison to put in his food and drink. The other suggested motive is to get rid of his rival, but I suspect Florence was all in the past and most unlikely for them to get together again. He had access to poison but no opportunity to administer it to Bravo.

D. Had Charles Bravo taken the poison, albeit possibly too much, to cause trouble for Florence and/or Jane Cox? Hence why he would not say what it was and raised tremendous suspicion against them and possibly Gully whom he detested. If so, then it all backfired on him. Why use antimony?

E. There was a belief amongst Victorian women how putting a small amount of antimony in their husband's drink would soon make him sick. The idea being to make him stop drinking too much and/or to ward off his sexual advances. Had Florence done this, but miscalculated the dose?

Florence was unusual in a period when women suffered from various discriminatory practices, such as not having the vote. Few had the luxury of marrying for love. Instead, especially in the upper classes, they married for security. Once married, they had to endure whatever their husbands wanted, including violence. As an added insult their husbands could take on a mistress with impunity, but if their wives returned the compliment, it was social suicide.

Some people call her radical, but whenever Bravo taunted her about Gully, she retaliated in kind about his mistresses. If she did murder him, it would be understandable but still illegal and if found guilty she would have hanged. Had that been the case, then she would have been wicked.

Despite murder not being proved, in her case with all the scandal, she would have been a wicked, wilful and unconventional woman in the eyes of Victorian society. Do you agree?

9
Sarah Chesham *née* Parker (1809-1851)

Born near Saffron Walden, Essex, Sarah was nineteen and pregnant when she married Richard Chesham in July 1828. Their daughter, Harriet, was born the following year and more children followed. A family of six must have put a tremendous strain on their slender financial resources. Richard was a lowly farm labourer with no prospects of doing anything which paid better.

Once their children turned five, they were sent out to work and bring some more money into the house. However, the Agricultural Revolution was in full swing and farmers were cutting employees rather than engaging any more. As this was not an industrial part of the country, working in factories and mines was not an alternative option.

Joseph (11) and James Chesham (8) became ill in January 1845 and were attended by Dr Hawkes, although no mention is made about how he would be paid. Despite his efforts, the boys died following severe vomiting and abdominal pains. Dr Hawkes thought they had both died from **English Cholera**, which was rife at the time. He signed their death certificates accordingly and the boys were buried in the same coffin at Clavering churchyard.

Solomon Taylor was the illegitimate son of Lydia Taylor who lived in the nearby village of Maunden. Evidence proved he was a healthy child at the time of his birth. Following visits from Sarah, his health quickly deteriorated with severe bouts of vomiting and abdominal pains until he died. The popular inference was Sarah had poisoned him. Consequently, she was arrested, and the bodies of Joseph and James were exhumed.

In March 1847, Sarah appeared at Essex Assizes, charged with the murders of Solomon Taylor and her two sons. Medical evidence confirmed the suspicions how all three had been poisoned by *arsenic*. In fact, there were three trials as she was tried separately on each murder.

There was no doubt, Joseph had been poisoned, but the Crown could not prove Sarah had administered the fatal doses. The jury retired for just ten minutes before finding her not guilty.

A fresh jury heard the case concerning James and came to the same conclusion.

The third trial also failed because there was no evidence to prove any poison had been administered to Solomon. Following on from this particular result, a case against local farrier Thomas Newport was withdrawn. He had been accused of supplying the poison to Sarah to murder Solomon, who was probably his illegitimate son.

These acquittals were not well received. As far as the locals were concerned, Sarah was an accepted and reputed murderer who had got away with it. There was little or no doubt in their minds she was guilty. It cannot have been easy for her to continue living amongst them, but she had no alternative.

Matters were made worse when in May 1850, Richard Chesham (43) died.

He had long since suffered from a lung disease, but his death had been accompanied with severe vomiting and abdominal pains. Almost immediately these symptoms rang warning bells, and although Richard had already been buried, his body was exhumed. Whilst this was happening, his, now Sarah's, house was searched by the police under the command of Superintendent John Clarke. Here they found a quantity of rice, which together with the contents of his stomach were sent for analysis.

No one was surprised when the rice and stomach contents were found to contain arsenic. It was well known how Sarah gave her husband milk thickened with flour or rice. She was arrested yet again.

This time when she appeared once more at Essex Assizes at Chelmsford, Sarah was charged with attempting to murder her husband. It was well known how only she fed him. It was probable the arsenic had killed him, but was it just the poison? Could it have been the lung disease or a combination of both? Remembering the previous acquittals, the Crown considered the charge of attempted murder would have more chances of succeeding.

Dr Hawkes, from Saffron Walden, testified to seeing her feed Richard with some milk which had been thickened with flour or rice. He added how she refused to allow anyone else to feed him.

Another witness, Hannah Phillips provided even more damning evidence. She told the court about a conversation with Sarah. The topic concerned Hannah's unhappy marriage coupled with Sarah's advice to murder her husband with arsenic.

Sarah gave a statement on her own behalf, which was not on oath, as that practice had yet to become law. Her denials failed to impress the jury who wasted little time in finding her guilty.

The judge was very biased against her during his pronouncing the death sentence. He referred to the other times Sarah had been tried, adding she had confessed to murdering her children! There is some doubt as to whether she made such a confession. Having been acquitted earlier, she had nothing to gain by doing so. She could not be tried again for those offences.

Clearly, he considered her to be a serial killer and had no hesitation in sentencing her to death. Sarah was transferred to Chelmsford Gaol on 24th March 1851 and kept her appointment with William Calcraft, hangman, the next morning. As she had only been convicted of attempted murder, her body was claimed by her son and buried in Clavering later that evening, but without any form of religious service.

Sarah Chesham had the dubious fame of being the last woman to be hanged in public at Chelmsford and the last woman to be hanged for attempted murder.

Author's comments

Was Sarah Chesham a wicked woman?

I believe Sarah was guilty and this was the correct charge. The judge's comments were made after the guilty verdict. But even if he had made them whilst summing up, there was no court of appeal and it would not have made any difference. There was enough prejudice and ill-feeling towards her to have influenced the all-male jury without his comments. Here was a wife charged with administering poison to her husband. How much benefit of the doubt would the jury have given her, because the evidence was circumstantial? I suggest none.

In any case, she still faced the death penalty for attempted murder.

What was the motive for wanting to murder Richard?

This is not clear cut. He was unwell but I cannot see her murdering him as an act of kindness: and certainly not with arsenic. I suspect it was because he had become a hinderance to her and was costing money, especially if not working and she needed to move on.

She had the means to do it with the arsenic, and her insisting on being the only person to feed him, provided the opportunity and strengthened the Crown's case. And arsenic more than enough for a fatal dose was found in her lodgings. Obviously, it was the means as proved by the remains found in Richard's stomach. But where is the evidence that she administered it? Undoubtedly, as she would not allow anyone else near him.

Being a married couple, there would have been no end of opportunities to administer the poison. Yet, why would she do it when the doctor was either present or expected? Was she just being brazen and possibly getting a thrill from it? Alternatively, could she have been fabricating an alibi by making him think feeding her husband was an innocent act.

Would the verdict be the same today based on this circumstantial evidence as only the means were satisfactorily proved? I would not like to say.

Returning to the first two cases concerning the death of her sons.

The means would appear to have been by arsenic and the opportunity arising from Sarah, as their mother, feeding them. But what was the motive? The only suggestion would be to have two less mouths to feed, but at the same time, their deaths resulted in less money coming into the house, assuming they were working. There was no suggestion of them being insured and murdered for the payout. It is also extremely doubtful if Sarah and Richard could have afforded the premiums. The evidence against her was circumstantial and the jury really had no alternative but to acquit her.

Solomon Taylor is different again.

This case was probably put together somewhat hurriedly in the mistaken belief the outcome would not matter, as she was going to be convicted of murdering her sons. The obvious motive would appear to have been for money, but that was as far as the Crown could go, and where was the evidence for it?

Being unable prove what had caused Solomon's death, as there were no signs of poison in his stomach, meant there was no evidence of means let alone opportunity.

However unpopular a decision it was, the judge had no alternative but to acquit her.

Having regard to all the above, Sarah's descendants took part in a television programme and have convinced the interviewers how she was wrongly convicted, and the case should be revisited. Their argument being it was not unnatural for people to have a small amount of arsenic in their bodies.

Nevertheless, looking at Sarah's history, I think she was a wicked, wilful and unconventional woman.

The last hanging in England for attempted murder was that of Martin Doyle at Chester in 1861.

10

Marie Corelli, *née* Mary, *aka* Minnie Mackay (1855-1924)

Marie was the illegitimate daughter of Dr Charles Mackay and his servant Elizabeth Mills. Being already married, he had to wait until his wife died before marrying Elizabeth. With such a complicated background, it is easy to see why very little is known about Marie's early days. To avoid confusion, she will only be called Marie.

She was sent to a convent in Paris in 1866 to further her education, before returning to Britain. Reports vary on how long she spent there. During the next few years, she indulged in a musical career giving piano recitals. It was probably during this period she began toying with the idea of hinting about having an Italian background. This re-invented Marie maintained she was a countess who had been abandoned on the Mackay's doorstep as a baby. After her father died in 1883, she took on the name of Marie Corelli adding to her claims of Italian ancestry.

There can be little doubt this was untrue, and in many ways sums her up as living in a fantasy world. Marie was also very vain and never admitted her real age, always saying she was *'around thirty.'* Whenever possible, she avoided having her photograph taken. When one appeared in her latest book, it had to be touched up to make her appear much younger than she really was. Marie always dressed like a teenager.

Music took up little of her time and in 1886, she published her first novel titled *A Romance of Two Worlds*. It could not be called a great success and was fiercely criticized. Writing in the Spectator, Grant Allen described her as 'a *woman of deplorable talent who imagined that she was a genius...*' Another critic described her as a combination of the imagination of Poe with the style of Ouida and the mentality of a nursemaid.

Poe is Edgar Allan and Ouida was the pen name used by Maria Louise Ramé. She was a successful writer who was born in 1839 and died in 1908.

Marie was totally unconcerned about such criticism as she believed in there being no such thing as bad publicity: only publicity. During the rest of her life, she had little or no time for the press. She once complained her name had been omitted from the list of guests at the Braemar Highland Gathering, accusing the publication of deliberately doing so. The publication confirmed she was correct, because of her contempt both for the press and those who wished to appear in it, who had been to society events.

Both letters were published in full in the next edition.

Many of her books contain a mixture of Christianity, **reincarnation** and **astral projection**, amongst other themes. Whenever critics savage other writers, perhaps it is because they are jealous. This may well have been the case with Marie. But whatever the reasons, she had the last laugh.

Amongst her many fans from all walks of life were Queen Victoria, H.G.Wells, Winston Churchill, William Ewart Gladstone, Edward Prince of Wales and other members of the Royal Family, to name but a few. By 1908, her annual income was £18,000 (approximately £1,400, 000 today).

During her time in London, Marie was regularly accompanied by Eric, her adored brother, but their relationship soured after he died in 1898. Some people now revealed how he boasted of having written her novels and not his sister. Marie was furious and accused him of all manner of trickery. Whilst nobody liked Eric when he was alive, they felt she was out of order in libeling her dead brother who was in no position to defend himself.

The whole business resulted in her leaving London and moving to Stratford-upon-Avon in 1899.

She had visited Stratford previously and felt this was the place to come with her long-term friend Bertha Vyse, sometimes called Vyvert or Vyver. It has been suggested she and Bertha may have had a romantic liaison, but this has never been confirmed. The suggestion was made following erotic descriptions of female beauty in some of her novels, although they made by men. She was known to have a passion for Arthur Severn.

Arthur was a talented water colour artist who she first met in 1906. He provided illustrations for one of her novels and a second project was planned on Shakespeare, which was finally abandoned in 1917. They communicated regularly but despite all her passion for him, it was not reciprocated. Her feelings ranged from infatuation, frustration and rage. In his turn, Arthur frequently belittled her success and finally married another woman. Marie finally admitted defeat and ceased working with him. It is possible he used her for his own financial reasons.

There can be little doubt she considered herself to be another Shakespeare. In fact. Marie believed she was his reincarnation. On arrival, she moved into Hall's Croft where Shakespeare's son-in-law Dr John Hall had lived. And right from the beginning courted controversy.

There was a school very near to Hall's Croft and it was not long before she was in confrontation with the headmistress. As can be imagined, living close to a school was not a quiet option. Marie demanded total silence from them so as not to interrupt her working. It was never going to happen and before long she had moved into what is known today as Marie Corelli House.

Typically, this was how she would spend much of her time in Stratford: either falling out with people or being a great benefactor. To be fair to her, Marie was passionate about Stratford and never deterred by her enemies. On the other hand, she had a First Class Honours Degree in Tactlessness which she achieved effortlessly.

Sometimes her good ideas and intentions worked against her.

One such occasion occurred when she produced a magazine called the *Avon Star*. It provided an ideal opportunity for her arch enemy, the Reverend Harvey Bloom who, despite his clerical background, possessed a very vindictive streak. He quickly published his magazine called *The Errors of the Avon Star*.

Ever conscious of her believing she was the new Shakespeare Marie took a special interest in Holy Trinity Church where the Immortal Bard was baptized and buried. When actress Helen Saville Faucit who died in 1898, it was proposed to erect a memorial to her close to Shakespeare's grave. Marie objected, and the idea was dropped. In 1903 she paid off the church's debts.

During the same year, Marie came into conflict with the American philanthropist Andrew Carnegie, about the siting of the new library in Henley Street. Marie was always against demolishing old property in the name of progress. If the library went ahead, it meant three old cottages would have to be demolished and she was totally against the idea. Letters went to and from the local newspaper and Marie was accused of wanting to buy the cottages herself which she could sell to the council, and the new building would be called the Corelli Library. She sued for libel and won the case.

Marie was awarded damages of one farthing (¼d).

Next morning, she found a cardboard farthing(s) pinned to her front door.

There was no such thing as second place where Marie was concerned.

If there was no chance of her winning any competition, then she would not enter it. For instance, in 1901 there was a grand regatta held on the Avon. She and Bertha entered with a superbly decorated punt with flowers all over it. Most people believed she would win, but then the Theatre announced their entry. This consisted of a highly decorated boat commemorating Cleopatra. Marie quickly accepted it was better than her entry, but how could she avoid a defeat? She simply withdrew her punt from the competition stating it had only ever been intended for display purposes.

In 1903, she continued her river interests with a vengeance and purchased a gondola complete with a Venetian gondolier to operate it. It was a very good in theory, but the gondolier spent more time in the Black Swan, *aka* The Dirty Duck than on board the gondola, so he was dismissed.

Amongst her many critics was the American W. T. Stead. He visited Stratford in early 1912 and met Marie. Clearly won over by her charm, he promised to print an apology for his previous hard words on his return home. Unfortunately, he sailed on the Titanic and was not one of the survivors.

In the same year, she changed her ***dogcart*** and two Shetland ponies for a Daimler motor car. Now she and Bertha rode around Stratford in style, complete with a special seat for her dog, Czar.

1917 was not a good year for Marie. Firstly, she lost her current gondolier when he was killed in action during the war: she never used the gondola again. Later on, her popularity began to wane, and it was not helped when she was fined £50 (approx. £3,000 today) plus costs for hoarding sugar.

When Marie died on Easter Monday 21 April 1924, she left everything to Bertha who had remained her constant friend. There were problems with the will after Bertha's death, and her house is now owned by Birmingham University.

Ironically, Marie's funeral in Holy Trinity Church was delayed because of Shakespeare's Birthday Celebrations, Wednesday 23 April, so the Bard of Avon really had the last laugh.

Her years in Stratford would never be forgotten, where she made friends and enemies. Amongst her many achievements were dining with Edward Prince of Wales: meeting and socializing with many of the leading personalities of the day. One of her crowning achievements was having Dame Clara Butt sing at a musical event she had arranged. Despite all the attacks by her literary critics, she was invited to Edward VII's coronation but they were not.

Other acts of her generosity including paying for poor children to visit Stratford. She helped to save Harvard House whose former owners were involved in the founding of Harvard University.

Marie's life is best summed up as a fantasy with a mixture of fact and fiction. Nobody is completely sure of her background. Was she part Scottish or part Italian? Her date of birth is correct, but why did she never want to be photographed and lying about her age? Was it just vanity or part of her encouraging the legends about herself?

An enterprising young man produced postcards of her from paintings. She went ballistic and took him to court to have them withdrawn from circulation. The judge found in favour of the publisher and they quickly became collectors' items.

She is buried in Evesham Road Cemetery, complete with an imposing statue which resembles an angel with a hand in the air. But look closely at it and you will see her back is towards Stratford…and…her raised hand looks like she is giving the town a V-sign.

Author's comments

Was she a wicked woman?

I really do not think so.

Was she wilful?

Undoubtedly. She was a strong character who would not take no for an answer, even if she had to change her activity as with the 1901 regatta. She might not always have been right but was never wrong. Likewise, she only had to admit defeat when the sugar and postcards court cases went against her.

Was she unconventional?

I think so, although eccentric would probably be more appropriate in her case. The mystery over her background, especially the Italian claims all add to this suggestion. To be a true eccentric as opposed to having mental problems, one needs money. There is no doubt she was wealthy. The whole affair of importing the Venetian gondola and gondolier would not have been cheap.

11

Mary Ann Cotton *née* Robson *aka* Mowbray, *aka* Ward *aka* Robinson (1832-1873)

Reports vary as to where Mary Ann Robson was born. Suggestions include Low Moorsley, near Murton and East Rainton. The only certainty is she was born somewhere in the Durham area.

Mary's parents raised her as a Wesleyan Methodist which was their religion. Her father was killed in a mining accident and she became the family's main breadwinner at the age of fourteen. By all accounts Mary was an attractive girl with no shortage of admirers. In 1851 she married William Mowbray, a miner, and they moved to Plymouth seeking work.

What happened next varies depending on which accounts are believed.

William and Mary had at least three children by the time they left Plymouth to return to the North. Another report says it could have been five. Regardless of exactly how many children there were, they all died. The cause of death in each case was recorded as *gastric fever*.

Deaths in infancy were common in the mid-nineteenth century, and with poor, if any sanitation facilities, stomach problems were rife. Doctors were expensive and out of many people's affordability. Forensic science, like the new police, was very much in its infancy. Consequently no one queried these deaths.

They had another child on their return to Northern England, but he died and so did her husband. The cause of death was gastric fever for the child and diarrhoea for William. It later transpired William had died soon after Mary took out a large life insurance policy on him.

Having had some previous nursing experience, Mary worked in a local infirmary, where she met, and later married George Ward, one of her patients. He died soon after their marriage in 1866, from gastric fever, having been treated with leeches attached to his body. Mary Ann blamed them and the doctors who prescribed such treatment, for her husband's death. The doctors were cleared of any negligence.

Mary married recently bereaved James Robinson in 1867, who came with baggage of five children. The children all died from gastric fever before the year was out. It is surprising, even allowing for a short life expectancy among infants, why no official questions were asked about these quick succession deaths.

Her husband was not so trusting.

Accounts differ as to the cause of their tremendous argument which followed the last child's death. One blamed it on James becoming aware how his wife was defrauding him: another maintained it was about his growing suspicions regarding the children's deaths. Suffice to say, after the row, he went to bed and left her downstairs. In the morning she had gone with all his savings and other valuables.

On the positive side, he kept his life.

Her next marriage came in 1870, when Mary bigamously married Frederick Cotton. He came with two sons, and she was also five months pregnant by him. Henceforth she was always known as Mary Ann Cotton. Only days before their wedding, her future sister-in-law Margaret Cotton suddenly died from gastric fever. This happened just after she had willed all her goods to Frederick, and his soon to be new wife Mary.

By July 1871, the family had moved to West Auckland following a dispute with their neighbours about some pigs which had mysteriously died. Two months later, Frederick died...from gastric fever. More family deaths followed with gastric fever being shown as the cause of death.

Never being one to let the grass grow under her feet, by Christmas, she was living with an old lover, William or Joseph Nattrass. This arrangement did not last long as he and young Frederick Cotton, were both dead, by 1 April, from gastric fever.

By now, the neighbours were starting to talk, although it is doubtful just how much they knew about her. Mary Ann did not help herself, as she was now pregnant by Mr Quick-Manning, the local excise officer and openly living with him.

But luck was running out for Mary Ann Cotton.

On 12 July 1872, her stepson, Charles Cotton died. Gastric fever once again was shown as causing his death.

However, only a very short time before his death, Mary had been approached and offered a new nursing position by Thomas Riley, a parish official. She agreed but needed to get young Charles out of the way. Her next move was to approach the local workhouse superintendent and tried to get the boy committed there. Her application was rejected, but hearing of the boy's death., which was just too coincidental the superintendent quickly told the police about her visit.

An *autopsy* was carried out on the boy's body, but not at the local hospital, workhouse, or cemetery. Little Charles was brought home, where he was opened up on the kitchen table. His stomach was found to contain *arsenic*.

Suddenly Mary Ann remembered and said how shortly before he died, she had found him licking the wallpaper. It was well known how nineteenth century wallpaper paste contained arsenic, as did most of the paint used on it. These claims were soon counteracted by a local chemist who had sold her arsenic, just before the boy's death, ostensibly for killing bed bugs. Some of her other victims were exhumed and their bodies found to contain arsenic.

Mary Ann Cotton was charged with murdering Charles Cotton, although the trial was delayed because of her pregnancy.

Her defence at Durham Assizes was simple.

The prosecution was conducted by Charles Russell, who also was involved in the Adelaide Bartlett and Florence Maybrick trials. Mary's defence maintained she had found young Charles licking the wallpaper, which contained arsenic in its paste notwithstanding the evidence she bought arsenic, shortly before his death. This defence might have succeeded, if it had not been for the evidence, introduced by the Crown, of the other members of her family who had been poisoned.

Her defence barrister objected they were not relevant to her one charge of murdering Charles. He was overruled, following the similar principles, accepted in the trial of Dr William Palmer, some twenty years previously. The jury took just forty-five minutes to find her guilty and she was sentenced to hang. There was an immediate outcry about hanging a woman, no matter how bad she was, but it was to no avail. She was not reprieved.

On 24 March 1873, Mary Ann Cotton kept her appointment with the hangman, William Calcraft, although he was now seventy-nine years old. He was not remembered for being one of the country's most efficient executioners and she did not have the easiest of deaths, struggling for at least three minutes.

In a matter of hours, children had produced a rhyme:

Mary Ann Cotton,
She's dead and she's rotten.
She lies in her bed
With her eyes wide open.
Sing! Sing! Oh what can I sing?
Mary Ann Cotton's tied up with string.
Where? Where? Up in the air,
Selling black puddens a penny a pair.

The author recently spoke to someone from Durham who can remember chanting this rhyme whilst she and her friends used their skipping ropes. For many years afterwards, Mary Ann Cotton became the demon every parent used to threaten their misbehaving children.

It will never be known how many victims Mary Ann Cotton had killed, as she never made a confession. It is thought to be in the region of twenty and may have included her own mother. For the most part, money was undoubtedly her motive. It was a question of either obtaining their life insurance money or just getting rid of children, who were in the way and costing her money. In between her marriages, she existed as an opportunist opportunist thief.

She was not a nice person to know.

Author's comment

Was Mary Ann Cotton a wicked woman?

The answer can only be yes. She was a cold calculating person who was only interested in money regardless of how she obtained it.

There can be no doubt her motive was to benefit financially from each death, even the children. She took out funeral plans on her children and husbands, then murdered them and claimed the insurance money. Insurance companies tended to pay out with very little or no checks performed.

Infant mortality rates were high and almost everyone suffered from stomach upsets. Diseases such as *cholera* were thought to be spread by smelly air and not contaminated water. In other words, these deaths would not have seemed too unusual except for their numbers, which caused her ultimate downfall.

The means was clearly arsenic. There would have been no shortages of opportunities to poison her victims. Arsenic was easily obtained, and her victims automatically trusted their mother, stepmother or wife who fed them.

She was very wilful and unconventional being only interested in her own well-being.

Regardless of whether or not you would want Mary Ann Cotton to be your daughter-in-law, I suggest you would not want to dine with her!

12

Marie Madeleine Marguerite de Brinvilliers
née d'Aubray (1630-1676)

Marie was born in Paris to the wealthy and well known Dreux d'Aubray. She was described as pretty with an air of *'childlike innocence.'* This latter description contradicts the suggestion she had been sexually abused and enjoyed an incestual relationship with one of her brothers.

As it transpired later, the term *'childlike innocence'* was most inappropriate.

On attaining the age of twenty-one, she married Antoine-Gobelin, Marquis de Brinvilliers (pronounced Branvillyers). He was a wealthy man to which was added her considerable dowry. Unfortunately, he was an unsuccessful gambler and the money had soon gone, leaving him deeply in debt.

They both indulged in affairs. One of hers was with Jean Baptiste Godin de Sainte-Croix. Their affair was blatant, scandalous and she spent lavishly on him. Meanwhile her husband had fled France to escape his creditors. Her father was not prepared for his daughter's scandal to continue and he had Sainte-Croix arrested and put into the Bastille for a year.

It was a move which had very unforeseen and diabolical consequences.

Whilst in the Bastille, Sainte-Croix met an Italian known as Exili, who was a poisoner. Very little is known about him although it is thought his real name was Nicolò Egidi. The two men became cell mates and in time, Exili passed on his knowledge of poisons to Sainte-Croix. Marie was waiting for him on his release, and together they plotted to murder her father. She opted to use an **arsenic** based compound known as **Acqua Tofana** after another Italian poisoner…Giulia Tofana.

Before her execution in 1659, Giulia had confessed to killing hundreds of men with her poisons. There is a possibility, she had been handed down the recipe by her mother, who was executed in 1635 for murdering her husband.

For the next eight months Marie experimented on her maid and patients in the local hospital. As her knowledge of poisons grew, she gradually dosed her father with small amounts of the acqua tofana. When he died in 1668, his cause of death was thought to have been from natural causes, and no suspicions were aroused. So far so good, but there was a big problem brewing.

She had no intention of sharing the unexpectedly small inheritance with her two brothers and sister. Marie now planned their deaths. It is quite possible she had already earmarked them for death, before realizing just how small her inheritance was, just to make sure of getting more money.

Undoubtedly what happened next ultimately caused her downfall.

Marie needed to ensure no suspicion fell upon her, so she employed a young man, Jean Hamelin, commonly known as La Chausée, to work in her younger brother's household. She paid him handsomely to continue her work and under instructions gradually set about murdering the two brothers.

Her eldest brother was given a glass of wine and water by his new valet, La Chausée. Having sampled the contents, he spat them out complaining: 'It burnt like fire.' The valet apologized and blamed another servant for pouring out the drink. So, the matter rested for a while.

In the following spring of 1670, he hosted a dinner party which resulted in all the guests suffering from suspected food poisoning. The vol-au-vents, supplied by La Chausée were blamed. Everybody recovered except d'Aubray, who later died.

Being mindful of the guests taken ill at the party, the doctors were suspicious and carried out a post-mortem, but found no traces of any poison. They described his death as being caused by malignant **humours**.

Her younger brother was later afflicted with a similar illness and died the same year. Another post-mortem took place. Whilst the doctors could not prove poisoning, they discovered ulcers on his lungs which were a clear enough indication it was not a death from natural causes.

Marie's sister now feared for her life. When it was suggested she took on La Chausée as a gardener, she declined to employ him knowing how he had been employed by her dead father and brothers. She also wasted no time in telling the police about him.

Meanwhile, Sainte-Croix had died.

There was little of any value in his estate, except for a small chest measuring about eighteen inches square. It was thought to contain valuables and a dispute arose over its ownership. Sainte-Croix's widow laid claim, insisting she was entitled to it. The other claimant, however, was Marie. Her association with the dead man was well known, and she had considerable influence at court.

A compromise was reached, and the box was opened in the presence of the two women and the police.

Sainte-Croix had instructed this box was only to be opened after his death if it happened before Marie. Possibly Marie suspected what was inside. She had promised him a considerable amount of money, which had not materialized. To say Marie was unhappy with this opening arrangement is an understatement.

The box was opened and inside were two papers involving money, which were possibly a clumsy attempt at fraud. But what was underneath them was more interesting.

These were several small parcels of powder. A sample was thrown on the fire where it burnt with a violet flame, which suggested poison. The powders were tested immediately by an alchemist and revealed as virulent poisons that left no trace.

But worse followed, when a bundle of papers was discovered amongst marked curious secrets.

Two names were also uncovered in the box, who were suspected of using or going to use the poisons. One was an extremely rich man named de Pennautier and the other: Marie Madeleine Marguerite, Marquise de Brinvilliers.

De Pennautier had known Sainte-Croix and was renowned for being ruthless. He was a very powerful individual who could and probably did buy his way out of any trouble. Suffice to say, he was never charged with any offence, but Marie was a different proposition.

She was short of money and her husband had none to help her. It did not take too long to remember all her previous scandals. Also remembered was her being short of money and the suspicious deaths of her father and brothers. For the moment, there was no direct evidence to connect her with those deaths, but that was about to change.

La Chausée had vanished, as he was not yet being sought for murder. Albeit he was not free for very long.

He was arrested by chance as a vagabond. When he was searched, a quantity of white powder was found on him, which he claimed was for sharpening razors. This powder was tested and proved to be the same type of poison that had been found in Sainte-Croix's box. La Chausée was also known to be an associate of Sainte-Croix.

After being tortured, La Chausée confessed to murdering Marie's brothers after being given the necessary poison by Sainte-Croix, who insisted Marie was not involved. La Chausée did not believe this and admitted as much. Meanwhile, Marie had taken refuge in a religious house, but kept an ear to the ground regarding how the enquiry was progressing. She soon heard about La Chausée's confession.

Worse news followed.

Marie was sentenced to death in her absence until such times as she was arrested. Meanwhile, she fled to Germany and entered a convent, depending on a very small allowance from her sister. For the moment she was safe as there were no extradition laws in existence. But the Paris police were determined to bring her back to France for execution.

Their agent, François Degrais was tasked with bringing her back, regardless of how long it took. He is described as having a 'gentlemanly appearance' which totally belied his lack of scruples and incredible iron will.

Once he had discovered where she was, he disguised himself as an abbé which enabled him to enter the convent. Here he carefully cultivated a friendship with Marie. Having once established how bored she was in the convent he suggested a ride out into the countryside and to take breakfast at a country inn. Marie could not agree quickly enough. But, instead of having breakfast, she was arrested by Degrais's men and quickly taken back over the border into France. It was quite an eventful journey as she had tried to commit suicide and arrange a rescue on the way.

She was questioned by the authorities and totally denied any involvement in the deaths of her father and brothers. Unfortunately, Degrais had found a confession in her handwriting, not only about the murders, but also about some of her other activities, which totally damned her.

This was at a time when Paris was rocked by the *Affair of the Poisons*.

Wealthy women were easily obtaining poisons, then murdering their husbands and other family members. They were part of a group which practiced black magic and participated in satanic orgies. Even one of Louis XIV's mistresses was involved and allowed her naked belly to be used as an altar. Marie was one of these women.

She tried to say these confessions were untrue, but no one believed her. However, it was felt it would help the prosecution case if she made a fresh one. It was arranged to put her to the water torture, but in the end it was unnecessary. Rather than be tortured, she made a full confession to the murder of her father and two brothers. Marie agreed to using La Chausée to kill her brothers and named a chemist who had obtained the poisons for her. The man was now dead.

In due course she kept her date with the executioner on 17 July 1676, ten years after her father's murder. On the way to the scaffold, she asked him to walk between her and '*the scoundrel Degrais*'. She is described as only wearing a shift but acting with great dignity amongst a very hostile crowd.

Her execution was drawn out as the executioner spent more than fifteen minutes cutting her hair so it would not spoil the sweep of his sword.

Author's comments

Was Marie a wicked woman?

Her motive was money and the means by poison. She undertook the poisoning of her father but used La Chausée to murder her brothers.

Undoubtedly her sister would have been next. With both murderer and victim living in the same household, there would have been no shortage of opportunities to administer the poison.

Regardless of just how ethical Degrais' methods may or may not have been today, it was much different in seventeenth century Paris, especially in a world where there was no extradition. In my view, Marie was a thoroughly wicked woman and perhaps the means justified the end to bring such a wicked, wilful and unconventional woman to justice.

How unconventional was she when compared with the women involved in *the Affair of the Poisons?*

Had Sainte-Croix not died so unexpectedly, this affair might never have come to light, although La Chausée could have been a problem. It also raises the question of Sainte-Croix's death. Was it an accident, caused by his unintentional inhaling of some poison? Or could it have been something more deliberate? Clearly Marie was concerned about what was to be found in his box, so had she decided to shut him up? Who knows?

13

Marie-Anne Charlotte de Corday d'Armont
(1768-1793)

Born in Normandy, Charlotte Corday, as she is usually called, came from a minor aristocratic family. Following the deaths of her mother and elder sister, her father was unable to cope, so he sent Charlotte to Caen with her younger sister. By 1791, she was living there with a cousin. According to her passport, Charlotte was just over five feet tall.

Having begun in 1789, the **French Revolution** was now moving towards the period known as the **Reign of Terror**.

Whilst living in Caen, Charlotte met many supporters of the **Girondins**, and became an admirer of their speeches. This was a period of great turmoil and power struggles amongst the various parties of the Revolution.

During September 1792, there were numerous slaughters of prisoners throughout France, not all of which were political. The actual numbers are not known but included many Girondins. One of the main instigators was Jean-Paul Marat who was a member of the radical Jacobin faction.

These were created by Maximilien Robespierre in 1789. Originally called The Society of Friends of the Constitution, which was soon changed to The Society of the Jacobin Friends of Freedom and Equality in Government. Known as the **Jacobins**, they advocated extreme violence against anybody who opposed their views.

This background, especially the earlier massacres, had a profound influence on Charlotte. She held Marat personally responsible for what had happened. She further believed if he continued unchecked, then civil war was inevitable. Charlotte also thought the execution of Louis XVI had been a mistake. In short, she believed Marat was a threat to the French Republic and he had to go, but not simply deposed. He had to die.

And she would attend to it.

On 9 July 1793, Charlotte travelled to Paris where she purchased a kitchen knife with a six-inch blade (15cms) and took a room in a hotel for a few days. Her original intention had been to stab Marat in front of the National Convention and thereby make a public example of him. She quickly realized this course of action was impossible because he no longer attended these meetings because of his health. He had contracted a debilitating skin disorder, possibly *dermatitis herpetiformis*.

The only treatment available to him involved spending as much time as possible in a bath, from where he conducted his affairs. Charlotte had to change her plans and went to see him there but was turned away. Undaunted, she returned in the evening claiming to have knowledge of a proposed Girondin uprising. Marat agreed to see her, and she was brought to him.

At first Charlotte gave him several names which he wrote down, but as he did so, she stabbed him in the chest. He cried for help and whilst a military surgeon and dentist tried to revive him, Charlotte's arrest followed swiftly.

It was soon apparent Marat was dead.

Charlotte's trial quickly followed.

She had asked for Claude le Doulcet, an old friend, to defend her but it seems he never received the letter in time. It has been suggested, though never proved conclusively, how the public prosecutor, Antoine Quentin Fouquier-Tinville delayed it. Her guilt was quickly established and on 17 July 1793, (just four days after murdering Marat), she was guillotined.

An individual working on the scaffold, named Legros, slapped her face after she had been beheaded. It is said how her face registered indignation at the slapping, which supported the belief how severed heads still have life for a few seconds after being removed. Legros was sent to prison for three months for this offence. Charles-Henri Sanson, the executioner, rejected any suggestion Legros was one of his assistants. He was a carpenter doing some work on the guillotine.

A post-mortem was carried out on her body in the belief she was co-habiting with another suspect. The Jacobins were dismayed to discover she was in fact a virgin.

In a letter to her father, Charlotte stated how she had avenged many innocent victims. Unfortunately, the murder of Marat did not achieve her aims and the Jacobins increased the Reign of Terror.

Author's comments

Was Charlotte a wicked woman?

Undoubtedly the Jacobins thought so as did many women.

Whilst Charlotte believed she acted for the best motives, did she really believe murdering Marat would change things in France? Clearly, she did, but it was a naïve belief. There was never any doubt about the subsequent means and opportunity of committing this murder. At this period in France's sad history, her trial was a mere formality and even if Le Doulcet had defended her, it would have made no difference.

If Marat had been the only person running France, his death might have changed matters. But it did not make any difference. Others took his place.

Murdering another human being does put her into the wicked category. And if it had not been Marat, would somebody else have done such as Robespierre or Fouquier-Tinville? It is not clear what attempts, if any, she made to escape from Marat's house, or was she quite prepared to become a martyr? Ironically, Marat was looked upon as the martyr: not Charlotte.

If Charlotte had escaped, what would have happened next? Would she have returned home or gone after the other leaders?

Robespierre remained in power for a few more months until he was guillotined in 1794.

Fouquier-Tinville was one of the most ruthless leaders during the Reign of Terror, nicknamed Purveyor to the Guillotine. He held on to life until 1795 when he went to the guillotine, as he had sent countless others. At his trial which lasted forty-two days, he claimed he was *only obeying orders*.

Where have we heard that one before?

In the grand scheme of things, Charlotte was not destined to win, and I must wonder a bit at her mental state? She would have us believe she acted from the best of motives and in her mind, Charlotte probably did. There is no doubt she was deeply affected by the massacres and felt something had to be done. Yet, with no back-up or other plans, I feel she was misguided, wilful and unconventional, as opposed to being completely wicked.

14

Christiana Edmunds (1828-1907)

Would you happily eat some chocolates or cake that suddenly appeared through the post, with no note or other indication as to who had sent them? You would probably treat them with a great deal of suspicion, but it was a different story in Victorian Sussex.

Christiana was the eldest child of William and Ann Christiana Edmunds. He was a successful architect responsible for the building of Margate Holy Trinity Church and the pier lighthouse, amongst other projects. She lived with her parents, two sisters and two brothers in Margate. A plain and unattractive girl, she had enjoyed few, if any male admirers, despite a privileged background and private boarding school education.

It had not been too easy a life in her younger days.

Her father died early in 1847 after he was certified insane and removed to Peckham House Asylum in South London. His death left the family in straitened circumstances. One of Christiana's brothers had been certified insane and also died in an asylum. Her other brother became a doctor, married and emigrated to South Africa. More tragedy followed when her sister Louisa married but died from unspecified gynaecological problems, although it has been suggested she might have committed suicide.

Unable to continue living in their comfortable Margate house, mother and her two surviving daughters moved to Brighton by 1867. Everything went well until 1869 when daughter Christiana consulted a doctor about her *neuralgia*.

Dr Charles Beard was aged forty-one and married with three children. By all accounts he was not particularly attractive, but for Christiana it was love at first sight which seems to have been reciprocated, albeit in an unusual fashion. A friendship now developed between the two families. Christiana was introduced to Emily Beard and their children. Their secret relationship consisted of numerous letters from her which were very amorous and implied how she wanted to marry him at a later date. Charles was very flattered by her advances and encouraged them with his own letters in increasingly passionate terms.

It has never been suggested their relationship was physical.

The problem, in Christiana's eyes, was Emily Beard. She knew there could be no future for her and Charles for as long as his wife lived. There was no doubt in Christiana's mind she would have to be removed, permanently, from Charles. Christiana began to plan her next move, in which Emily's death was her main intention.

One evening during September 1870, Christiana came to call, knowing Charles was away. Not suspecting anything untoward, Emily invited her in. Here Christiana gave Emily some poisoned chocolate creams and waited whilst she sampled one, taking care not to taste any herself.

Emily bit into it then prompted spat the chocolate out complaining about its bitter taste. Running out of the room she was violently sick. On her return, Christiana had gone and taken the chocolates with her. Later that evening Emily suffered from acute stomach pains. She told Charles about it and he immediately suspected what had happened. He challenged Christiana who denied being involved. Nevertheless, he broke off any further communications with her.

He did not report her to the police.

Probably Charles knew if he did, then his so-called affair with her would be made public. If that happened, there was no guarantee he would survive the ensuing scandal.

It was a decision which had tragic consequences.

Christiana was not going to be prevented from continuing their affair so easily and planned her next poisoning venture. She needed to prove the next batch of poisoned chocolates had nothing to do with her. Once Charles realized this, she reasoned, however illogically, he would believe in her innocence and all would be well again between them.

Her plan was simple.

All she had to do was show the chocolates had been purchased innocently with no blame being attached to her.

Christiana's first move involved her purchasing **strychnine** from local chemist, Isaac Garrett, Queens Road, under the pretext of destroying some feral cats. Next, she purchased chocolates from confectioner J. G. Maynard (no connection with Maynard's Sweet Company) of West Street. She was careful not to be seen purchasing them herself, so used local children to do so on her behalf. Once she had the chocolates in her possession, Christiana inserted the strychnine and returned them to the shop on the pretext they were not what she wanted. The shop exchanged them for other chocolates, and in this way the poisoned ones were sold on.

Christiana was not a chemist and her doses of strychnine did not have any real pattern to them. Consequently, not everyone who purchased the chocolates was affected by them. Some people were immediately deterred by the smell and left them alone. Others became ill but recovered.

The tragedy came when Charles Miller purchased some but did not like their taste, so he gave one to his four-year-old nephew Sidney Albert Barker, who ate it. He was immediately violently sick and died soon afterwards.

A post-mortem revealed strychnine caused the child's death, and an inquest was summoned. Christiana ensured she was one of the witnesses called. She claimed being ill after eating one of Maynard's chocolates. Despite her best efforts to blame him for the poisoned chocolates, the coroner's jury returned a verdict of accidental death without any blame being attached to him.

Christiana was furious her attempt to blame Maynard had failed so miserably, but she was not yet finished. Her next move was to write three anonymous letters to Sidney Barker's father recommending he sued Maynard for the death of his son.

He ignored them.

Changing tactics, Christiana wrote to Charles imploring him to resume their affair, but he declined.

Christiana would still not take no for an answer and started on her next poisoning campaign. Having discovered how strychnine left a smell, she changed tactics and now used **arsenic**. Realizing there was no way Maynard would supply her with any more chocolates, Christiana changed to poisoning cakes and fruit.

Her plan now involved sending anonymous parcels of cakes and fruit to various people including Emily Beard. Unlike other Brighton residents, she did not eat them immediately, but saved them for a weekend treat and probably saved her life in doing so. Brighton residents were suddenly being taken ill after receiving anonymous presents of cake and fruit.

Charles now realized what was happening and he went to the police with his suspicions.

They had already been investigating the poisoning cases and Christiana was one of the complainants. She was interviewed by Inspector Gibbs who already had his suspicions about her. During the interview, she made a show of spitting out some alleged poisoned fruit in his presence, but it was to no avail. A quick comparison of her handwriting alongside the labels on the poisoned packages confirmed she was the culprit and not a victim.

Her arrest and trial followed.

Originally scheduled to be heard at Lewes Assizes, the venue was moved to the Old Bailey because of fears of a biased trial if heard locally. Feelings ran high against her and she had already been burnt in effigy.

She pleaded not guilty and the trial began on 15 January 1872.

During the second day, evidence was produced regarding the insanity in Christiana's immediate family and on her mother's side. A medical specialist testified to her being on the border between being a criminal and insane.

The jury was not impressed and found her guilty of the murder of Sidney Albert Barker. Sentence of death followed.

Their verdict caused even more outrage because it was generally thought Christiana was insane and not responsible for her actions.

Christiana was reprieved and sent to *Broadmoor* for the rest of her life, where she died in 1907.

Throughout her time there, Christiana never appeared obviously insane nor did she display any psychotic tendencies. Also, she never showed any understanding or regret about her crimes and no attempts were made to obtain her discharge. Even though she was not actively suffering from any mental illness, it was felt she remained a risk to public safety.

Ironically, Dr Beard finished his days in a lunatic asylum.

Author's comments

Was Christiana a wicked woman?

If she really was insane, she would not have been responsible for her actions and therefore not wicked. Nevertheless, she was and remained a dangerous woman who could never be released into the community. She was certainly calculating enough to think of the exchanging chocolates ploy and using children to make the initial purchases. And there was her campaign to put all on the blame onto Maynard.

Was she wilful?

Given her mental state, there cannot be any clear-cut answer. Perhaps a dangerous woman might be a better description

Was she unconventional?

It can be argued her actions were, but how influenced were they by her mental state? Charles Beard must take some responsibility here. He encouraged her infatuation with him, but why? Was he flattered by it? Did he think it was just a bit of fun? Was his married and professional life so humdrum he was flattered by her attention and actively encouraged it?

He was only too aware of the risks to himself and his career and possibly marriage which decided him not to go to the police after the first attempt on Emily's life. Had he done so, Sidney Barker might not have died, and Christiana would have been taken out of circulation as a serious public danger much earlier.

With such a family history of insanity, it is little wonder she went the same way.

Another unanswered question is how much did Emily know about his affair with Christiana?

From the jury's point of view, it was a clear-cut case.

Her obvious motive was to remove Emily from the scene to enable her to marry Charles. True, she had not meant to specifically kill Sidney Barker. But as far as she was concerned, Sidney and anybody else who was poisoned, were collateral damage in her main plan.

The means was by way of the poisoned chocolates innocently supplied by the confectioner.

Her opportunity came with the unsuspecting people who purchased the poisoned chocolate. She was completely reckless as to who suffered provided she got Charles back into her life.

I wonder how many of the people who objected to the jury's verdict lived in Brighton.

15

George Eliot *née* Mary Ann Evans *aka* Cross

(1819-1880)

Mary Ann, sometimes known as Mary Anne or Marian, was born in Nuneaton, Warwickshire. Her father, Robert, was the manager of the Arbury Hall Estate for the Newdigate family. She was born on the estate but soon moved into Griff House, between Nuneaton and Bedworth.

Whilst she was not considered physically beautiful, Mary was a keen reader and obviously intelligent. Her father was aware of his daughter's lack of physical attraction and believing she stood little or no chance in the marriage market, ensured Mary received a good education. He sent her and older sister, Christiana, known as Chrissey, to a boarding school in nearby Attleborough and other establishments in Nuneaton and Coventry.

Leaving school at sixteen, she received very little further formal education, but thanks to her father, Mary had full access to the Arbury Hall library and continued her self-education. Here she immersed herself in Greek literature which had a profound influence on her subsequent writings.

These visits to Arbury Hall had an unexpected consequence which would influence the rest of her life.

She began contrasting the different lifestyles between the wealthy landowners and their much poorer tenants. Another important part of her early days was living in the Midlands with its growing number of different religions.

Her mother died in 1836 and her beloved married brother, Isaac, took over the family home. Mary moved in with her father to act as his housekeeper and they moved to nearby Foleshill. Living so close to Coventry it was inevitable Mary not only maintained her contacts there, but also increased them.

Two of these were Robert and Caroline Bray. He was a very wealthy ribbon manufacturer and owner of the *Coventry Herald* newspaper. As well as being a radical thinker, he used his money to build schools and tried to better the lot of the poor. Their house, Rosehill, became a regular meeting place for many of the radical and free thinkers of the day. Amongst them were Robert Owen, a great social reformer and Mary.

Rosehill was a popular place to debate radical and social matters, including religion. Much to her father's dismay, Mary began questioning her own religion. His daughter's views upset him so much, he threatened to turn her out of the house. Unwilling to upset him, she moderated her opinions in his presence, and acted as a dutiful daughter.

Nevertheless, she continued associating with the Rosehill Circle and wrote various articles, some of which Bray published. When her father died in 1849, she travelled to Switzerland with the Brays and stayed on after they returned home. She left there in 1850 and moved to London with the sole intention of becoming a full-time writer.

Initially she lodged in John Chapman's house. He was a publisher she first met at Rosehill, and who had recently purchased the *Westminster Review*. This was a left-wing publication and fitted in well with his views. Now calling herself Marian Evans, she began writing various articles which he published. These concentrated on the plight of the lower classes and criticism of religion, much of her background knowledge came from her time on the Arbury Hall estate.

It is unclear what her romantic involvement was with Chapman. When she moved into his house, he was already living there with his wife and mistress!

Some of her other views were just as radical.

For instance, Marian sympathized with the European revolutions of

1848, although she advocated a more gradual reforming policy would be preferable in England.

Later, following the outbreak of the American Civil War, she supported the North in contrast to the majority view in England of supporting the South,

Some historians believed slavery caused the war in 1861. In fact, Abraham Lincoln did not order all slaves to be freed until 1863. It is often argued how their emancipation was a political measure, to prevent England entering the war on the side of the South.

Marian was a supporter of Irish Independence.

Between 1851-1854, Marian became the assistant editor of the *Westminster Review*, although she did most of the work. This was when she met George Henry Lewes and they decided to live together.

Described as a philosopher and critic, Lewes was already married to Agnes Jervis in what was described as an '*open marriage arrangement*,' whereby she had children by any man she chose. In 1854, she had three children from Lewes and a further four from other men.

The couple went to Germany, officially for research, but treated it as a honeymoon and now referred to themselves as Mr George and Mrs Mary Ann Evans Lewes.

Whilst Mary was more than happy with the arrangement, her brother Isaac was not. As head of the family, he felt he should have been consulted at the very least and been asked permission for George to marry his sister. Most annoyed, he made enquiries and was scandalized to discover George was already married: but not to his sister. Whilst extra-marital affairs were preferably conducted with discretion, George and Mary made no secret about themselves. In retaliation, Isaac banned the rest of the family from contacting her. Mary was devastated but her love for George overcame it.

Later she was reconciled with Chrissey.

She and George struggled financially and not just because of their own living expenses.

They also had to support Agnes and her growing band of illegitimate children. None of her lovers contributed anything to their upkeep. During this time, Mary moved away from radical articles to writing novels. These were initially serialized in *Blackwood's Magazine.*

Founded by William Blackwood, this magazine appeared between 1817-1880, and was well established when Mary's first fiction appeared in it. Although women wrote in the Victorian era, most were not regarded very highly. Mary was aware of these prejudices and adopted the pen name of George Eliot. George came from her lover and Eliot for no other reason than it was a simple name.

1859 saw the publication of her first complete novel, *Adam Bede,* which was set in the fictitious Warwickshire town of Milby. It was an instant success, helped by the mystery surrounding its author. North Warwickshire residents quickly realized Milby was based on Nuneaton, but who was this mysterious George Eliot? Clearly it was a pen name and they tried to discover his true identity. There was at least one pretender who claimed to be George Eliot before her real identity was discovered.

The revelations about her liaison with Lewes shocked most of her readers.

Yet, despite her publisher's worries, Mary's popularity did not decrease. Nevertheless, neither Mary nor George were accepted into society until 1877, when they were introduced to Princess Louise. Her mother was Queen Victoria. It soon transpired the queen was an avid reader of Mary's novels. If the couple were accepted by Queen Victoria's family, society had to change its attitude.

Sadly, they did not have long to enjoy this sudden change in their fortune.

In fact, Mary had written her last novel, *Daniel Deronda,* in 1876, and they moved to Surrey because of George's declining health. He died in November 1878 and Mary was totally devastated. The only comforting presence she had was from Charles Lewes, who was George's youngest son.

Mary spent the next two years finishing George's final work, *Life and Mind,* and found companionship with John Walter Cross. He was twenty years younger than Mary and handled all her financial affairs. They had known one another for many years and married in 1880.

They were not surprised when this marriage caused another scandal on account of their age difference. But Isaac was delighted she was now legally married, and it led to a happy reconciliation between her and the rest of the family.

Mary and John honeymooned in Venice, but it was not straightforward.

John had to be rescued after being found in the Grand Canal. It has been suggested it was a suicide attempt when he jumped from their hotel balcony. Other reports state how he fell into the water. Whatever the truth of the matter he survived, and they returned to England. They moved to a new house in Chelsea, but Mary soon contracted a throat infection, which was aggravated by her long-term kidney disease.

She died just before Christmas 1880.

Westminster Abbey was suggested as an appropriate burial place for such a talented, albeit controversial writer. Supporters of this idea were not surprised when the dean objected to the idea. There were no such problems in Highgate Cemetery where she is buried alongside the love of her life... George Lewes.

On the centenary of her death in 1980, a memorial stone was erected in Poets Corner at Westminster Abbey.

She is also well remembered in and around Nuneaton, e.g. the George Eliot Hospital.

Author's comments

In the eyes of hypocritical Victorian England, there can be little doubt she was considered wicked.

The fact many men had mistresses was acceptable, provided they used some degree of discretion. Once such arrangements became common knowledge, social disproval followed. Isaac was not a forgiving brother whilst her liaison with George lasted. Only after his death and Mary was legally married would he accept her again back into the family. It seemed he was not influenced by his sister being accepted by royalty.

Undoubtedly her radical views and opposition to some forms of religion would not have made it easy for him. Would Mary still be regarded as wicked if she had been born a hundred years later? With a much more relaxed attitude to people living together out of wedlock, I doubt it. Perhaps she would be better called a modern woman as opposed to a wicked one.

Was she wilful?

Mary did what she wanted to do regardless of who she upset in the process. She must have known living with George would cause problems within her family. Likewise, the company she kept in the *Rosehill Circle* upset her father.

I think she was wilful.

Whatever doubts there might be about her being wicked or wilful, there can be no denying she was unconventional. In many ways Mary was way ahead of her time and not deterred by her gender. When looking at her life, there really seems to be very little conventional about her.

For instance, look at her marriage.

For an unattractive woman, she had some sex appeal, yet why marry John when there was such an age difference between them? And there is the whole unanswered question of how he came to be in the Grand Canal. There is no suggestion she pushed him, but at least one report states he was suffering from depression. On his honeymoon? What had caused that? Had he realized the marriage was a mistake?

We shall never know, and it all adds to the diverse character of George Eliot.

16

Seymour Dorothy Fleming *aka* Worsley

(1758-1818)

Seymour was the youngest daughter of Sir John Fleming, 1ˢᵗ Baronet of Brompton Park in Middlesex. When he and two of her sisters died in 1763, Seymour and her elder sister were brought up by their mother. She remarried Edwin Lascelles, 1st Baron Harewood in 1770. He was a wealthy sexagenarian whose money came from his West Indies plantations.

In complete contrast to Seymour, her elder sister, Jane, Countess of Harrington, was renowned for being a paragon of virtue.

On 20 September 1775, aged seventeen, Seymour married Sir Richard Worsley, 7th Baronet of Appuldurcombe House on the Isle of Wight. She was now styled as Lady Worsley until his death in 1805. Although she was supposed to bring £70,000 (approximately £6,457,837 today), on her marriage, it was probably nearer £52,000 (approximately £4,537,275 today), which was still a considerable amount of money.

No doubt it was an arranged marriage which began falling apart almost immediately. The couple only had one child, Robert, who did not live very long. There was a later daughter, Jane Seymour Worsley, who was born in 1781. Although Jane bore the Worsley name, Richard was not the father. He claimed Jane was his to avoid a scandal.

Her real father was Maurice George Bisset, and soon after Jane was born, Seymour eloped with him.

Bisset was a captain in the South Hampshire Militia and had been Richard's friend and neighbour on the Isle of Wight. Richard was furious by this turn of events and he sued Bisset for £20,000 (approximately £1,722,000 today) for *criminal conversation*, which was another name for adultery.

The subsequent trial of Worsley vs Bissett in 1782 was a very scandalous affair with all manner of revelations.

The court was told how she had, apparently, some twenty-seven lovers, although Bisset was her main one, who was being sued. Bissett defended the accusations and she helped his defence with the aid of several past and present lovers. In doing so, she questioned the legal status of her husband. Many of her lovers testified to their sexual relationship with Seymour. There was some suggestion Worsley was a *voyeur* who encouraged these arrangements, obtaining his own sexual gratification by watching her have sex with other men.

One witness was Doctor William Osborn, who had treated her for venereal disease, which she contracted from one of them. With so many lovers and imperfect contraception devices, it is a wonder she only contracted it once and did not conceive again.

Her affair with Bisset happened after Worsley helped him watch his wife whilst she was taking a bath. Bisset had sat on Worsley's shoulders. This revelation resulted in a popular cartoon of the day showing the two men and Fleming. It destroyed Worlsey's case. In other words, he had encouraged Bisset to take a sexual interest in his wife.

Despite all this evidence, the jury awarded him damages…one shilling (approximately 5p today).

Had they found fully in Worsley's favour, there is no way Bisset could have paid the sum of money the other man was seeking. He depended on Seymour for money. Nevertheless, in many respects it was a pyrrhic victory.

Following these revelations in court, there was no way Worsley could live with her as his wife. Both she and Bisset hoped a divorce would happen, but he would not agree, but arranged for a separation instead. Acting this way meant she could not now marry again until her lawful husband died. Worsley controlled her purse strings which effectively cut Bisset off from any easy access to money.

He left her in 1783.

Seymour had no money of her own and the only way she survived depended on the favours she was given by becoming a professional mistress to rich men. She was not alone in these circumstances. Such upper-class women were known as *The Female Coterie* and Seymour became one of them.

During this time, she had four more children, one of whom was by Bisset. By now she was heavily in debt and fled to France to escape her creditors.

It was not the best time to be in France as the **French Revolution** commenced in 1789. It is believed she was imprisoned during the **Reign of Terror** but returned quietly to England in 1797. Soon after coming home, Seymour became seriously ill.

The illness brought about a reconciliation with her mother, sister and brother-in-law, which enabled her to return to Brompton Park. This had once been hers, but she was prevented from holding by the property laws of the day.

This was how she lived until 1805 when her husband died. As an added bonus to his death, she received a *jointure* of £70,000, (approximately £3,000,000 today), which had been the agreed dowry she brought with her, irrespective of whether or not Richard Worsley had been short changed.

It was now time for her to move on, which she did only a few weeks later when she married her current lover, John Lewis Cuchet. He was twenty-six years old whilst she was now forty-seven years old. In the same month, she resumed her maiden name of Fleming, by royal licence which her new husband took.

On 30 May 1814, the Treaty of Paris ended the War of the Sixth Coalition against Napoleon who was then exiled to the Island of Elba. Seizing the opportunity to leave England, Seymour and John moved to Passy in France where she purchased a villa. The Hundred Days War following Napoleon's escape from Elba, did not affect them and they lived here until 1818 when she died.

Author's comments

Does Seymour rate as being a wicked woman?

It can be argued how despite coming from a privileged and titled background, she was bundled into an arranged marriage with a man who was totally unsuitable. She would not have sought the union herself, and no doubt her stepfather was responsible. Seymour was only twelve years old when he came into her life and was just too young to marry off then. But as soon as she was seventeen or almost there, it was time for him to get rid of her. Granted it cost him money, but he could afford it. It was not a match made in heaven and soon unraveled, which is why Seymour sought comfort in the arms of Maurice Bisset, whom it would appear was the first of many lovers. As Bisset's trial revealed, and if the evidence can be believed, she had at least twenty-seven in the first seven years of her married life. And more followed.

Following her separation from Worsley, she needed to exist and there was no help coming from her family. Consequently, she used the charms of her body to survive, albeit being very choosy in the process. Seymour was not the first nor the last woman to act in such a way.

Does such a hyper sex drive make her wicked? Perhaps she can be considered a ***nymphomaniac*** or perhaps suffering from a mental disorder rather than wicked?

Undoubtedly her critics will maintain she was a wilful woman and they would be right. Seymour gave the impression of doing what she wanted. Or was she driven to do it this way by force of circumstances which affected her life?

She was unconventional and acted in a manner in complete contrast to how she was expected to behave. By arranging for her lovers to testify in the court case Seymour ensured her own notoriety.

Perhaps Seymour was a mixture of wicked, wilful and unconventional. She was certainly a complex character who broke the rules of polite society.

Her exploits haven't been captured on film in *The Scandalous Lady W.*

Joshua Reynolds painted her portrait between 1775-1776. It shows her wearing a striking red riding habit adapted from the uniform of Worsley's

Regiment, which he painted soon after her marriage. The painting hangs today in Harewood House, which was built for Edwin Lascelles. It can also be seen, albeit fleetingly, in the *Downton Abbey* film of 2019.

17

Mary Ann Geering *née* Plumb (1800-1849)

Mary was born in Westfield, East Sussex to agricultural labourers. Being the eldest of five children, she kept house for the family. At the age of eighteen, Mary went into service where she met and later married Richard Geering. Three months later, the first of their several children was born.

It was not a happy marriage.

Richard was the bread winner whilst Mary raised the children. Things started to go wrong in 1846 when he was left the sum of £20 (approx. £1,400 today). For reasons never really explained, he deposited this money in the Hastings Savings Bank and gave the passbook to his sister for safe keeping.

Why did he not give it to his wife?

About this time, their eldest son, William's wife died and he plus his three children and moved back to his parents' home.

During September 1848, Richard was taken ill and died five days later. The cause of his death was recorded as heart failure and the matter was soon forgotten.

Then, four months later son George (21), was also taken ill. He suffered serious attacks of vomiting and sadly died.

Just six weeks after the funeral, his brother James (26) was taken ill with the same symptoms and died soon afterwards. Only a few days later, his brother Benjamin was taken ill with the same symptoms. He was attended by two doctors who removed him from his mother's care and he soon recovered.

This rapid recovery started alarm bells ringing, and suspicion immediately fell upon Mary with the belief he had been poisoned. And, if he had been poisoned, it was highly likely his two brothers and father, who experienced similar violent vomiting, had been murdered in such a fashion. The coroner ordered the immediate exhumation of Richard, George and James Geering. An inquest jury was quickly sworn in and they all proceeded to the churchyard where the three men were buried.

Richard's coffin was removed first, placed on a tombstone and opened.

Unfortunately, it had been in a watery part of the churchyard and needed drainage holes drilled into it before the body could be examined. Richard's body was in such an advanced state of decomposition, his face was totally unrecognizable. Luckily, help was at hand with the coffin maker who was also the sexton. He readily identified the coffin as the one which had contained Richard's body. This evidence of identification was accepted by the jury.

George's face was recognized and identified. But James had to be identified by his coffin in a similar manner to his father.

The stomachs of all three bodies were found to be in an excellent and unusually good condition and were sent for analysis. As Richard's stomach was being removed, a small white piece of gritty substance was found, which resembled *arsenic*.

The inquest was adjourned to await the results of the analysis. Nobody was surprised to learn arsenic had been discovered in all their intestines. Meanwhile, as the evidence of poisoning was so strong against Mary, she was remanded to Hastings Gaol. Her case was not helped following the discovery of arsenic in her house.

On 6 August 1849, Mary pleaded not guilty at Lewes Assizes to the murder of her husband and two sons plus the attempted murder of a third son. She was described as '*a woman of masculine and forbidding appearance.*'

Witnesses testified to seeing Richard taken ill on two occasions after he had eaten food prepared by Mary.

Benjamin told the court about the symptoms he had seen on his father and two brothers. He added how his father and a brother belonged to *burial clubs* (although this is doubted in some reports), to provide money for their funerals. Other Geering children were unaware of any reason for Mary to keep arsenic in their home.

The doctor, who had attended Richard, remembered Mary telling him her husband suffered from a family complaint of heart disease. His treatment had proceeded accordingly, and he agreed it was the cause of Richard's death adding a bilious intermittent fever. Following Richard's death, Mary insisted the coffin lid was screwed down quickly, before any mourners could look at him. She had also been heard wishing her husband was dead on other occasions.

There was no doubt all three had been poisoned: two with arsenic and George with *mercury,* which she had purchased in Hastings. Likewise, the contents of Benjamin's stomach, which he had vomited, were found to contain arsenic.

It appeared the money which Richard had inherited was the probable cause of his murder and they regularly quarreled over it. No doubt this was why he gave the bank book to his sister for safe keeping. Mary had wasted no time in drawing it out following his death. The main part of her defence was what little remained plus any money from the burial club, would barely have paid for the funeral costs.

The jury were not convinced and after retiring for ten minutes, returned verdicts of guilty on all charges.

Sentence of death followed, and Mary was led away remaining as unmoved as she had been throughout the proceedings.

A space of three consecutive Sundays was customary before the hanging was carried out on 21 August 1849. During this time, she made a full confession admitting the murders. An estimated crowd of 3000 to 4000 watched her demise. Her executioner was not recorded.

Author's comments

Mary Ann Geering is not one of the more widely known poisoners. Undoubtedly, she was one of several people, usually women, who abused the burial club system.

There can be little doubt she was wicked, wilful and unconventional, and

I can find only one redeeming features in her case, which was her confession before her execution. Not that it changes my opinion of her.

She had the motive, which was for financial gain, despite her protestations to the contrary. The means she used were arsenic and mercury. The opportunity was at any time because the victims all lived under her roof and she nursed them. As such, she was someone whom they should have trusted i.e. mother and nurse, who was tasked with looking after her charges: not murdering them.

18

Frances Evelyn Greville *née* Maynard *aka* Darling Daisy and Countess of Warwick (1861-1938)

Popularly known as Darling Daisy, Frances enjoyed being Countess of Warwick and she had another nickname, of *Babbling Brook*. This came about because she could never keep a secret. It was very much a pun on her husband's name of Lord Brooke. By upper class Victorian marriage standards, it worked despite her spending money as if it was going out of fashion. The only cloud on the horizon was the threat to world peace caused by Kaiser Wilhelm II in Germany.

That was until one morning in 1914, when she went to her favourite store in nearby Royal Leamington Spa.

Her good mood was soon shattered when she was greeted by the proprietor, who announced bluntly: '*I am afraid my Lady, there is nothing in this store that is suitable for you to buy.*'

With her cheeks burning, Daisy had no alternative but to return home to Warwick Castle. She knew, only too well, what the man had really meant. It had nothing to do with him not having any stock. The unspoken message was he was not prepared to serve her, because of all the money she owed him. This was a real problem for Daisy.

The one thing she did not have was money.

Daisy knew there were all manner of treasures back in the castle, but they were not hers to sell. In any case, the castle finances were not exactly brilliant, and she and the earl rented it out during the summer to the wealthy Americans Henry Wheelwright Marsh and his wife, Agnes. It is also doubtful how far the sale of these treasures would have gone towards settling her debts.

At that moment, they were in the region of £100,000 (approximately £6,000,000 today), not that she had a clue about money.

She believed everybody was rich and nobody was poor. Consequently, she never had any qualms about spending money, and most of her purchases were on credit. Her creditors regularly submitted their invoices, but all she did was to put them away in a drawer, along with countless others. If something took her fancy, she would acquire it. One such fancy involved the purchase of a baby elephant and two emus.

Daisy's parties were very much sought-after affairs, not just in society: but in high society. At the end of the nineteenth century, your wealth and standing meant nothing if you were not on her invitation list. She spared no expense and her guests had to do likewise, or never be invited again.

For instance, in 1895, she held a '*bal poudré*' or '*powdered ball*' at the castle.

Marie-Antoinette was one of Daisy's favourite characters, and this event replicated a ball she had held in pre-Revolution France. All the guests had to attend in authentic late eighteenth century French clothing complete with accurate hairstyles. There were not enough hairdressers in England who had these skills, so Daisy imported some from France.

As Edward Prince of Wales, (later King Edward VII) was attending, she dressed as Marie-Antoinette. Her gown, along with other dresses cost in the region of £110 (approximately £9,600 today). Daisy proudly wore a fur mantle costing £800 (£66,000 today), which she lost. There are photographs of this ball on display in Warwick Castle.

The problem Daisy now faced was how to solve her financial problems, and here she was most resourceful.

Daisy was an attractive woman who had never lacked male admirers and bed mates. Her husband accepted the situation, which was common enough amongst the nobility. Many marriages took place for financial reasons, not love, with the wives being required to produce an heir and a spare. When they had done that, the wives were free to live as they pleased.

Everybody knew what was happening.

At many week-end house parties, two rising bells were rung in the morning. The first one was to get everybody back to their own bedrooms before the second bell, when the maids brought round the tea. Yet, whilst sexual infidelity was accepted, falling in love with your bed mate was not.

One of Daisy's lovers, and undoubtedly the best known, was Edward, Prince of Wales. He was a formidable womanizer and Daisy fell nicely into becoming another one of his mistresses. Whatever Daisy's husband might have felt about the arrangement, he accepted it. After all Edward was destined to be the future king, so even if he wanted to, what could the earl have done? Probably not very much.

Remembering their earlier relationships, Daisy started planning on how to resolve her financial problems: and she knew just how to do it.

Despite knowing the first golden rule about not falling in love with your bed mate, Edward did just that, and Daisy had the evidence to prove it.

During their time together, Edward had written several letters to Daisy, and in one of them he described her as '*our lovely little Daisy wife*.' Edward had died four years earlier and would not be affected, but she reasoned the Royal Family would not want these letters to be made public.

Edward's many affairs had been an embarrassment to them, and his son, now George V would prefer these letters never to see the light of day. Their revival would only upset his mother and Daisy reasoned they would happily pay her a hefty sum of money to prevent that happening. She chose Arthur du Cros to act as her agent.

He was both a friend and one of her many creditors. If it meant he had a chance of getting his money back, or some of it, he probably did not need much persuading. It is doubtful if she told him the full story, especially her back-up plan if things went wrong.

Waiting in the wings was James Thomas Harris (1856-1931) better known as Frank Harris. Described as an '*irascible and aggressive character*,' although born in Galway, he was now a naturalized American. Always a restless individual, he obtained a law degree but soon became bored with litigation matters and turned his attention to writing. He is best remembered for his highly explicit novel *My Life and Loves*, which was banned in many countries.

As negotiations proceeded slowly between du Cros and the Palace, she let it be known Harris had already bought the letters from her with the intention of publishing them in America. She reasoned the Royal Family would not want that to happen and would pay her what she wanted. True she had Harris waiting in the wings but had not yet sold the letters to him.

In fact, Harris was in some trouble and had taken refuge in one of her properties. His pro-German views in the current political climate did not endear him to many people at home and abroad. Undoubtedly, he used some of this time to read the letters, and quickly realized what a goldmine they were. Whilst he waited, Harris wrote several specimen chapters of his proposed book, but the ongoing threat of war meant no one was interested in publishing them.

Daisy had not realized how the Palace could also be devious. They told her they would buy the letters but kept stalling on the actual details.

Then Fate took an unexpected hand.

On 28 June 1914, The Archduke Franz Ferdinand of Austria and his wife, Duchess Sophie of Hohenberg, were assassinated in Sarajevo by Gavrilo Princip. A few weeks later, on 4 August, Great Britain was at war with Germany. Suddenly Daisy's letters ceased to be so important, except in one respect which caught her completely unprepared.

The Palace acquired a temporary injunction against Daisy which prohibited her from disposing of the letters. In all her scheming, she had overlooked one very important fact. Although she might be in possession of these letters, she did not own their copyright. That had stayed with Edward, passing down to George V on his death. In other words, they were not hers to sell and, in theory at least, she should surrender them to the Palace.

Still defiant, Daisy announced she was going to publish her memoirs which would undoubtedly include details of her affair with Edward. But Fate intervened again in the form of D.O.R.A, or more correctly, The Defence of the Realm Act 1914. One of its provisions made any attack on any member of the royal family a treasonable offence. Publishing these letters or even a part of them, would fall into this section.

Daisy now had two choices: to shut up or be shut up. It was no contest. The letters were not going to be purchased by the Palace nor be published and she was still left with an enormous debt. With all her plans having gone astray, how could she resolve it?

Using all her feminine charms, she turned to du Cros and begged for his help which he readily gave. Forgoing the money which she owed him, he helped Daisy find other means of settling her debts. He really had very little choice in the matter. She had made it quite clear there were sections in the letters which did not show him up in a very good light. It was blackmail and he knew there was no chance now of him ever recovering the money she owed him.

This was only the beginning and he found himself giving her more and more money. Coupled with him paying off some of her other creditors, Daisy kept away from bankruptcy.

But there was still the threat of legal proceedings against her, the Earl of Warwick, Frank Harris and others. The action was halted on condition she surrendered the letters to the Palace to be destroyed. Still fighting she tried her charms on George V, but was soundly rebuffed. Hereafter the whereabouts of the letters and what happened next, remain a mystery. I suspect du Cros had a hand in returning them to the Palace, which might explain his sudden knighthood in 1916.

Ironically, losing her fur mantle in 1895, turned Daisy to politics.

After the ball she was fiercely criticized for her expenditure and challenged to do something about it. However, her growing financial difficulties and the First World War, delayed any further progress for several years. When the country had settled down after 1919, she turned to socialist politics. To be fair, she visited many wounded service personnel during the war and helped entertain them.

It is not too difficult to imagine what her fellow socialists thought about attending meetings at the castle: somehow not really the image they wished to project. The proof of the pudding came at the General Election in 1923, where she stood as the prospective socialist candidate for Warwick and Leamington Spa. Not that it did her chances any good. She lost heavily to the conservative candidate who also happened to be her daughter's stepson-in-law.

His name was Robert Anthony Eden, who would later become prime minister.

One could be forgiven, perhaps, for thinking her close brush with bankruptcy would have taught her something about money. It was not the case.

When she died in 1938, Daisy had a vast collection of tropical birds. She left over 500 of them to her long-suffering housekeeper in her will. It cost £8 (approximately £400 today) a week to feed them. The poor woman obviously did not have any access to such amounts of money and sold off the birds.

Author's comments

Was Daisy wicked?

No doubt many people felt that way and her activities certainly highlighted the difference between the upper and lower classes of society. Even an ordinary dinner party for her would cost far more than the average annual earnings of a working-class family. Clearly the episode of the letters taught her nothing.

This specific instance shows Daisy at her worst.

Her peers happily made excuses and stressed what a charismatic character she was. Nevertheless, Darling Daisy showed in her relationships with du Cros just how ruthless she could be. Blackmail was her weapon of choice against the Palace and du Cros. If he did return the letters to the Palace it cost him a considerable amount of money, then he deserved his knighthood. Women do not always have to kill to earn the title wicked.

Even if we disagree about her wickedness, she was a wilful character.

Whilst it is easy to think of her as being unconventional today, would she really have been so in her lifetime amongst her peers?

The episode of the letters highlighted how she could be quite a devious and determined person. Every time she was thwarted, Daisy came up with alternative plans until the Palace finally gained the upper hand.

19

Emma Hamilton *née* Amy Lyon
aka Hart (1765-1815)

Originally known as Amy Lyon, Emma, as she is referred to in this chapter, was born in Cheshire. Her blacksmith father, Henry, died mysteriously when she was just two months old. She was raised by her mother and grandmother but received no formal education. Henry had married Mary Kidd after a brief courtship in June 1764. It has been suggested his death might have been suicide following local gossip concerning him and his wife. Murder has also been suggested, but he might have died from natural causes at the age of twenty-eight.

Emma formed a long-lasting bond with her grandmother, but in 1777, she started work as a maid in Chester. This employment did not last and later the same year she went to London, still in domestic service. One of her fellow maids wanted to be an actress and Emma soon decided she wanted to go on the stage.

This also was a short career, and we find her next employed as a model and dancer at premises known as *The Goddess of Health* or *The Temple of Health* for a Scottish **quack doctor**, James Graham. He provided very expensive treatment for infertile couples to help them conceive. In return they had the use of his special bed through which gentle electric shocks were provided. They were also treated to mirth, pleasantries and everything else designed for their pleasure. Hence models and dancers. Today he would have called himself a sex therapist or a sexologist.

In 1780, Emma met Sir Harry Fetherstonhaugh, pronounced Fanshaw, who employed her for several months as a hostess and entertainer at his numerous parties. Her speciality was dancing in the nude. Although she was technically his mistress, he ignored her for much of the time, preferring to hunt and drink with his friends. If he was happy to ignore her, they were not, and this was when she got to know Charles Francis Greville (1749-1809). He was the second son of the then Earl of Warwick and Member of Parliament for the town where he owned the Rose and Crown.

Fetherstonhaugh, was far from happy in July 1781 when Emma told him she was pregnant. Having a pregnant mistress and future illegitimate children had no place in his way of life and Emma was quickly pushed out of it.

With no one to turn to, she approached Greville who readily agreed to have her as his mistress, but on one condition. She could not keep her child. Emma had no alternative but to agree. Her daughter, called Emma Carew, spent some time with her great grandmother, before being fostered in Manchester. Emma jnr kept regular contact with her mother until she became a governess and moved abroad.

Having disposed of Emma's child, Greville now set about educating his new mistress. He insisted she lived a modest life, dressed in subdued clothing and kept away from high society. As an added incentive, he had Emma's mother, now known as Mary Cadogan, join them as his housekeeper and chaperone. Just like Pygmalion's Professor Higgins, he taught Emma to speak elegantly and invited his friends around to meet her.

However, he insisted she was to be known as Mrs Hart.

Always short of money, Greville introduced her to the artist George Romney who was looking for a new model and Emma was ideal. He painted several studies of her which sold well, and Greville enjoyed a commission from them. These showed her in a variety of poses, both dressed and in the nude. She soon became well known in the best society circles as Emma Hart.

It was too good to last.

Money problems loomed prominently in Greville's life and he desperately needed to find a rich wife. He found one in Henrietta Middleton, but Emma was a big problem. Henrietta made it quite clear, she would not agree to marry him if he continued living with Emma.

Yet again, Emma would have to go and Greville had a devious plan to do just that. Emma was never consulted and remained blissfully unaware of what he planned until it happened.

He persuaded his uncle, Sir William Hamilton, British Envoy in Naples, to take her on as his mistress. This would leave Greville clear to marry Henrietta and relieve Hamilton of continually financing his nephew. He stressed how she would make a very pleasant mistress for his uncle and when the time was right, he would come to Naples and reclaim her.

Sir William (55) was recently widowed and lacked female company. He was currently in London and knew of Emma's beauty, thanks to her portraits. He was also a collector of beautiful objects and needed little persuasion to add her to his collection. Back in Naples Sir William was renowned for his hospitality but lacking a hostess he quickly realized how Emma would fill that role nicely.

In 1785, Greville suggested Emma went to Naples for a prolonged holiday because he had lengthy business to transact in Scotland. Emma happily agreed, believing the reason for her going to Naples was for her mother's benefit who had recently suffered a stroke. She was unaware Sir William had paid all their expenses.

Emma had no idea of the real reason behind her going to Italy.

Although only just turned twenty-one, she quickly realized the trip to Naples was a ploy to get rid of her. Once her anger had subsided, she settled down and enjoyed her new life. Then, instead of taking her as his mistress, Sir William began to court her, and she responded. Meanwhile they lived openly together with her mother in the same house, which limited some, but not all of their social engagements.

They returned to England in 1791 for the specific reason of getting married in St Marylebone Parish Church. He was sixty whilst she was twenty-six. She now became Lady Emma Hamilton. Two days later they returned to Naples. Whatever Greville might have planned for her, this was not what he had expected. He tried to make Sir William financially responsible for Emma Carew, who was now his stepdaughter.

Sir William ignored the request.

Lady Emma quickly settled into upper society life in Naples. In addition to speaking fluent French and Italian, she became a close friend of Queen Maria Carolina, who was Marie Antionette's sister. Amongst Emma's many talents, she was a very good amateur singer. During these early days, however, she is best remembered for her *Attitudes* which were living tableaux.

She was the main participant and portrayed herself as a living sculpture or painting. Some imitated the portraits which Romney had painted of her and she wore the same clothes. For other events, her dressmaker made garments which were modelled on loose fitting local peasant clothes. These were accompanied by shawls and veils in which Emma draped herself but left very little to the imagination.

William loved the idea and her opening night, so to speak, was in 1787. The evening was a sensation and a new fashion began. Her *Attitudes* became a mime art. Life was good for Emma.

But it was all set to change irrevocably on 10 September 1793 and she would step into the realms of notoriety.

This was the date when a certain Horatio Nelson arrived in Naples and lost his heart to her. Although he only stayed for five days, as wife of the British Envoy, Emma spent some time in his company. The fact he was already married to Fanny Nisbet and had been so for six years had no bearing.

Despite being married to William for four years, they had no children and he was probably sterile. Although she regarded him with affection, he would never agree to Emma Carew coming to join them, as her mother's niece. And he would not make any enquiries in England to find her a suitable husband. For some reason he did not like the girl and probably equated her too much with his nephew Charles Greville.

When Nelson returned to Naples following his victory at the Battle of the Nile in 1798, Emma was delighted to have the opportunity to see him again. Within the week, she had become his secretary and fallen in love with him.

It was impossible to keep their affair secret, and soon everybody knew about it, including Nelson's estranged wife. Fanny now read about her husband's naval exploits along with graphic details of his personal life. But, as far as England was concerned, Nelson was defeating the French and could do no wrong in their eyes.

William seems to have tolerated their affair. His health was failing and all he was mainly interested in retiring. In many ways he could no longer compete with his wife.

Emma had become a serious political advisor to Queen Maria Carolina, no doubt helped and influenced later by the mail she attended to for Nelson. She had acted as a go-between in 1795 when her activities helped to prevent Naples falling into French hands.

William finally retired in April 1800. He, a pregnant Emma, her mother and Nelson travelled to London together where they took suites at Nerot's Hotel, much to the delight of the newspapers. Whilst William seemed to happy with this arrangement, Fanny was not. And, Emma was winning more hearts and friends than Fanny.

Nelson went back to living with Fanny, but he did not stop seeing Emma.

In 1801, he was promoted to Vice Admiral and returned immediately to active duty. As he prepared to leave, Fanny told him he had to choose between Emma or her. Nelson chose Emma and began separation proceedings from his wife.

Only a few days later, Emma gave birth to their daughter, Horatia. Nursing a baby was not for her and she quickly employed a wet nurse for this purpose and soon returned to the social scene.

For propriety's sake, they stated Horatia had been born in Naples and was their godchild. Nelson later stated Horatia was an orphan who had been entrusted into their care. The child was christened at St Marylebone Parish Church as Horatia Nelson Thompson.

Soon afterwards, Emma had a problem when George, Prince of Wales, and later king, became infatuated with her. Nelson was far from happy with this unexpected and unwanted turn of events, and he became very jealous. Sir William became involved and in an amazing letter wrote to Nelson assuring him of Emma's faithfulness.

Meanwhile, Nelson's family had taken to Emma, where she was a great help. She used her own money, or more correctly, Sir William's, to help with their education and weddings.

By late 1801, Nelson borrowed the money to purchase Merton Place, a house near Wimbledon, allowing her to renovate the property. Soon Nelson, Emma and her mother lived in this house, where they were joined in due course by Emma Carew. This was the first Nelson knew about Emma's older daughter, because she had not wanted to tell him. He took to the girl immediately and undertook financial responsibility for her.

In April 1803, Sir William died in Emma's arms and his creditors closed in.

As an executor of the estate, Greville was furious when he saw the extent of the debts Emma had incurred. He had expected to receive a hefty inheritance himself, only now there was not going to be so much for him to receive. There was no way he would give Emma any money. Also, Sir William had played down her role in Naples during 1795 and claimed most of the credit for himself. Thus, the government did not know she had done anything to earn a pension. She was for the moment totally dependent on Horatio.

More difficulties followed.

Emma allegedly gave birth to a daughter in early 1804, who died just a few weeks later. She kept this news from Horatio and there is no record of the girl's birth and death. Keen to keep all this from Nelson's family, she began gambling, spending money heavily and running up debt. Her health began to cause problems as she continued refurbishing Merton Place. It continually cost her money which she did not have. She declined several offers of marriage from wealthy men, steadfastly believing Nelson would become rich with all his prize money.

Following a brief visit in August 1805, Nelson returned to sea. Whilst away he wrote her a letter which was intended to be a codicil to his will. He requested the government to make ample provision to maintain her rank in life. This was to be in return for his service to King and Country.

On 21st October 1805, Nelson was killed at the Battle of Trafalgar.

He had requested Emma to sing at his funeral, but it never happened. Likewise, she was excluded from attending it with only men from the family doing so.

It did not take long for Nelson's family to exclude her. His son inherited most of the estate, (except Merton Place), £2000 (approximately £88,000 today) and an annual pension of £500 (approximately £22,000 today). Relationships between them worsened and Emma's brother blackmailed her for undisclosed reasons. She fought the government over the supposed codicil to Nelson's will, but nothing was changed. Meanwhile, she continued with her lavish lifestyle pushing herself further into debt.

Between 1811 and 1812 she was compelled to live in rooms within a three-square mile area of the debtor's prison with Horatia. It was a virtual extension of the prison. Emma had no money and she was unable to sell Merton Place. She tried petitioning the Prince of Wales, but unsurprisingly he declined to help, no doubt remembering how his earlier infatuation with her had ended.

In July 1814, she and Horatia fled to France and tried living another expensive lifestyle in Calais, but she was soon deeply in debt and had to move into cheaper accommodation. By January 1815, she was suffering from *amoebic dysentery*, probably contracted in Naples. Heavy drinking and *laudanum* consumption would have accelerated her organ failure.

Emma died on 21 January 1815 aged forty-nine.

Her actual grave has been lost following wartime bombardments, but she is commemorated by a plaque in the Parc Richelieu. Emma had been a popular person in Calais during these few short months, and all the Englishmen living there attended her funeral.

Horatia never publicly admitted being Emma's daughter. She subsequently married a vicar, had ten children and died in 1881. Her first child had the Christian names of Horatia Nelson.

Author's comments

Was Emma Hamilton a wicked woman?

No doubt Fanny Nelson and the government of the day probably thought so, which might explain why they carefully ignored Nelson's pleas to look after her. His openly living with her, and not being married, would have given them the perfect opportunity to save money. Yet, whilst he was alive, they were happy to accept him, faults and all, but not once he was gone. Now they left their one-time great hero to the history books.

Was she a wilful woman?

There can be little doubt she certainly was in her early days. She needed to be in order to survive, yet having once met Nelson, he became her one true love. Just how this worked with Sir William is anyone's guess.

Despite all the help, both financial and physical, she gave Nelson's family, they were quick to distance themselves from her once Horatio was killed. Now they had money of their own and did not need her. I think they only tolerated her whilst she was financially useful to them. Had she inherited Nelson's estate, I wonder what their attitude would have been then.

There is little doubt she was a good-time girl who, in her comparatively short life, had gone from rags to riches and back to rags again.

She was an unconventional woman and needed to be in order to survive. Not just with her pursuit of pleasure but it was unusual for a woman to have been so involved in politics in Naples. Sir William used her to his advantage by taking credit for what she had done. It can be argued he used her to further his own career, but had he told the truth, who would have believed him? A woman doing all this good work? Never! These were the late eighteenth and early nineteenth centuries.

Having married Sir William, she was entitled to be called Lady Hamilton, but in 1800 she acquired the title of Dame Emma Hamilton as a female member of the Order of Malta, in recognition of how she had helped in the Island against the French. Both the government and Sir William conveniently overlooked this award.

We know Nelson and Sir William visited Warwick in 1802, where the great hero was treated royally and pulled around the town by local men, instead of by his coach horses. The chances are Emma would have been with them.

Horatia's relationship with her mother is a strange one.

Nelson clearly did not want to acknowledge her as his own flesh and blood, hence the story of adopting her. Possibly society might not have condoned such an admission, and she did not acknowledge Emma as her mother. Was she ashamed of her and her antics? Quite possibly. It would not have been an easy childhood for her.

20
Prudence Hancox (?-1899/1900-?)

Very little is known about Prudence Hancox except she had a sharp temper and was very easily riled. When this happened, her fiery tongue came into play with a vengeance. She always wanted her own way and became a formidable enemy if it did not happen. Living in the Warwickshire village of Tysoe, most people knew of her and avoided the bad-tempered dressmaker. Not everyone was prepared to put up with her tantrums.

The Reverend Francis Dodson, Phillip Berridge, Seton Burn and Winnifred Turner were such persons.

It is not recorded how Phillip and Prudence met, but during 1899 they developed a relationship although she was ten years his senior. Doubtless there was no end of head shaking and gossip in the village about them. All went well in the beginning, but it was too good to last, and her true vitriolic nature soon appeared.

Phillip was appalled by her unpleasantness to his friends. Presumably they would have talked about it, but Prudence ignored his pleas and continued to offend him. To make matters worse, Phillip had become very friendly with Miss Seton Burn, who was employed by the Reverend Francis Dodson as a governess at the vicarage. Their friendship only made matters worse between the couple. Nobody was surprised and probably relieved when Phillip jilted her.

Apparently, Prudence had been taken by surprise, but she was determined to win him back by any means possible. Despite her efforts, Phillip had seen through her tantrums and kept well out of her way. By August 1899 Prudence realized she was getting nowhere when she heard how Phillip and Seton were planning to get engaged.

Prudence determined to win him back by spoiling his romance with Seton, in whatever way it took. Her hate campaign began in earnest.

Her initial strategy was to undermine Seton's position with the vicar, hoping she would be dismissed and leave the area. Prudence did this by writing a series of anonymous letters to him making all manner of scandalous allegations about Seton. She also sent other abusive letters to Seton and Phillip trying to upset their romance.

Whilst the recipients had little doubt Prudence was their author, they had no means of proving it. Despite her letters, Phillip and Seton's romance continued. Furious with the vicar for not dismissing Seton, Prudence now turned her full attention to him.

Firstly, she accused him of committing various crimes and paying Phillip £100 (approximately £7,800 today) to marry Seton. Still her tactics failed to work, so Prudence changed her plan and she verbally abused the reverend gentleman on every possible opportunity. It was a big mistake on her part.

He was not prepared to take any more of it and took her to court.

The first Prudence knew about it was when she received a summons to appear at court. Absolutely furious, she ran to the vicarage, but his servants had been well briefed, and they stopped her entering. Prudence contemptuously threw the summons at them and stormed home.

She duly appeared in court and was fined. Unlike today, the details of her slanderous remarks were not reported. If Phillip, Seton and the Vicar thought that was the end of the matter, they very quickly discovered it was not.

Within twenty-four hours Prudence was back at her letter writing.

Her first move was against the vicar once more, when she tried to stop him preaching but failed. Soon afterwards she turned her attention to Seton. In one letter, she called her *'a master sweep's daughter'* and enclosed some black bristles which had been cut from a broom. The inference was Seton had a dark complexion. Winnifred Turner was next with allegations of her committing all manner of unspecified crimes against the poor whom she nursed. Finally, Prudence started up a campaign to have Phillip run out of Tysoe for generally being immoral.

This was the last straw and her victims all went to the police.

In due course Prudence was arrested by Sergeant Street of the Warwickshire Constabulary. Admitting nothing, she continued protesting her innocence and tried putting the blame onto another woman in the area, also called Prudence Hancox. She complained also about receiving similar letters. But Sergeant Street was not convinced, and he carried out a thorough search of Prudence's lodgings, which was most rewarding.

Amongst the items he found, was an exercise book with loose pages, all of which were similar to the paper used for the letters. He also found some blotting paper which when he held it up to a mirror had no difficulty in reading some of the writing. The words were the same as on the anonymous letters. His last find was a broom from which some black bristles had been cut.

Importantly, what he did not find were any of the anonymous letters she claimed had been sent to her.

Sergeant Street was a thorough investigator who went a stage further and employed the services of Thomas Henry Gurrin. He was a renowned handwriting expert often consulted by Scotland Yard and the Bank of England. On checking a specimen of Prudence's handwriting against some of the letters, he was adamant her handwriting was the same.

Prudence appeared at Warwick Assizes in July 1900.

No one was surprised at her arrogance when she pleaded not guilty and sat impassively whilst the witnesses gave their evidence.

Winnifred could suggest no reason for being sent such letters. Phillip admitted being attractive to women but denied he and Prudence had been close. However, after receiving his first letter, he had discussed the matter with Prudence who dissuaded him from going to the police.

As she was now permitted to do so since 1898, Prudence testified on oath on her behalf. Her answers were very vague when she was cross-examined, usually consisting of '*I can't remember*' or '*I don't know*.' When questioned about the exercise book, Prudence maintained she had loaned it to someone who had returned it minus some pages. When pressed for the friend's identity, maintained it was a Miss Wilkes who had since left Tysoe.

She explained the missing broom bristles had been used by Mabel Pargiter to repair an ornament. Mabel was called as a witness, but she had no recollection of using any bristles in this manner. Throughout, Prudence continued claiming to have received letters herself alleging the police had not been able to find them. Finally, the judge was persuaded to let her go back to Tysoe and retrieve them.

Accompanied by Prison Warder Annie Stinchcomb and Police Constable George Barrett, Prudence returned to Tysoe the next day. George and Annie were instructed not to do any searching themselves but leave it all to Prudence. However, they were further instructed to watch Prudence very carefully all the time.

They had not been in the lodgings very long before Annie saw Prudence put a pencil and some paper into her pocket. Before they realized what was happening, Prudence rushed to the lavatory and tried to lock the door but was too late. Annie was the first one into it and saw Prudence beginning to write a letter to herself. Abandoning any further search, they all returned to Warwick without any further delay.

Annie testified as to what had happened and she was followed by George Barrett. When asked if there had been any other poison pen letters received in Tysoe during this period of Prudence's being remanded in custody, following her arrest, he replied '*no*.'

The jury retired for less than thirty minutes before returning a verdict of guilty.

For the first time, Prudence started to show signs of remorse when she heard the judge sentencing her to twelve months in prison.

Author's comments

Was Prudence Hancox a wicked woman?

I think she was probably more stupid than wicked. Possibly her mental state might have been called into question. She evidently considered herself to be above suspicion and the law, which clearly was not the case. Prudence would probably have received a shorter sentence if she had pleaded guilty and not tried to manufacture evidence.

She was certainly wilful, unconventional and a law unto herself. Being fined for the abuse she gave the vicar, did not act in the least as a deterrent.

Expert handwriting evidence is not new, being first used in legal proceedings during the third century AD. It has made tremendous advances since then.

21

Elizabeth Hervey *née* Chudleigh, *aka* Pierrepont, Duchess of Kingston, *aka* The Countess of Bristol (1720-1788)

Elizabeth was born to Colonel Thomas and Mrs Chudleigh. He was the Lieutenant Governor of the Chelsea Hospital, and believed to have lost his money in the **South Sea Bubble Affair** of 1720. Moving to Devonshire, he died in 1726, leaving his wife and daughter in straitened circumstances.

Despite her financial difficulties Mrs Chudleigh ensured Elizabeth received a good education. With the added advantage of being beautiful, intelligent, witty and charming, Elizabeth experienced no trouble in making friends. Good luck favoured her when she contracted smallpox in her mid-teens, it did not blemish her face

Thanks to one of her many friends she met William Pulteney, Earl of Bath. He took to her and it has been suggested they were more than just friends. Through his influence Elizabeth became a Maid-of-Honour to the Princess Augusta of Wales in 1743. Whilst the position came with an annual salary of £400 (approximately £47,500 today), it had a very strict proviso. Along with the other maids, she had to remain a spinster. Should she marry, an automatic dismissal followed.

She soon had many suitors, one of whom was James Douglas-Hamilton, later the 6th Duke of Hamilton.

It was a love match and the couple were adamant they would marry, but there was a problem. Not only about Elizabeth losing her salary, but James was about to embark on his **Grand Tour** and did not want to announce their impending marriage until his return. Elizabeth agreed and they pledged their love, promising to write to each other on a regular basis.

Whilst living in London, Elizabeth was under the guidance of her aunt, Mrs Cranmer, who was always searching for means of furthering her niece's prospects, and no doubt her own. She had decided Elizabeth could do better than young James and put her plan into immediate operation.

She intercepted all the letters which James sent to her niece and did the same with Elizabeth's ones to him.

Just as she had planned, Elizabeth soon believed James had found someone else. If that was the case, then Elizabeth no longer felt any attachment towards him. It was now time for Mrs Cranmer to put the next part of her plan into operation.

Such a chance occurred in 1744 at Winchester Races, where Elizabeth was introduced to Royal Navy Lieutenant Augustus John Hervey. It is unclear if he was the man earmarked by Mrs Cranmer or not.

Whilst Elizabeth's aunt is often regarded as being the real cause of their relationship, it should be remembered Hervey was a serial womanizer, sometimes referred to as the 'English Cassanova' because of his colourful life. Not that it would have mattered as Elizabeth was a headstrong woman, always with an eye to the main chance. Whatever the truth, Elizabeth and Augustus were married.

The ceremony took place in a little church at Lainston, just outside Winchester, shortly before midnight. Apart from the happy couple and Mr Amis, the vicar, the only others present were Mr Mountenay, the best man, who had a lighted taper in his hat; Elizabeth's aunt; her maid, Anne Cradock, and another unnamed person. At this time, wedding groups could dictate the time and place where they wanted the ceremony to take place: and the vicar had to agree. If marriages were secret, the bride and groom chose deserted parishes where the participants were not known.

Theirs was a secret marriage with no record being made, which suited them.

Firstly, Hervey knew his family would not approve and the marriage might cause problems with his naval career and seriously upset his finances.

Should this happen, the couple would depend on Elizabeth's salary, which she would lose on marriage.

Hervey was the son of the Earl of Bristol, and had a chance, albeit small, of succeeding to the title and all the wealth which came with it. Although not the first heir, his chance increased when the Earl died and Hervey's elder brother succeeded to the title. As a bonus, the new earl suffered from poor health.

However, Hervey's marriage to Elizabeth was not a happy affair.

After a four-day honeymoon, he was recalled to his ship and went to sea for several weeks. On his return, their re-union did not go well. At some stage there was a child who sadly, did not live very long. The big unanswered mystery was how did Elizabeth manage to keep her pregnancy secret from the other women at court? The couple grew apart, each taking lovers. Hervey was very experienced in such matters.

Although Elizabeth asked him for a divorce, he always refused.

In fact, Hervey had tried to persuade her to make their marriage official, but she always declined, probably ever mindful of the impending loss of her salary and independence should she do so. To make matters worse for him, she flirted openly with other men at court and behaved quite scandalously.

On one occasion at a ball held in Somerset House for the Venetian Ambassador, she appeared as **Iphigenia** and her dress, such as there was of it, would never be forgotten. It consisted of such scanty material which revealed most of her figure. Whilst the men were delighted, the women were not. The Princess of Wales draped her own stole over Elizabeth's shoulders. Possibly Elizabeth acted in such a manner to embarrass her husband.

Then the Earl of Bristol, Hervey's brother, became seriously ill and there was every chance he would die. From pleading with Hervey for a divorce, she now found it essential to be recognized as his wife, in the event of him succeeding to the title. For this to happen, the marriage needed to be officially recorded and the only person who could do that, was the Reverend Amis.

Elizabeth had him found but was only just in time as the man was on his death bed. He wrote out a certificate of marriage which Elizabeth delivered to Lainston. It was probably the last thing he ever did.

So far so good, but the Earl of Bristol recovered, and about now Elizabeth became the mistress of Evelyn Pierrepont, 2nd Duke of Kingston. Her life with him involved moving from one scandal to another. And now, Hervey approached her asking for a divorce so he could remarry. As he had refused all her previous requests for a divorce, Elizabeth took her revenge and refused to agree.

At some stage, James Douglas-Hamilton returned to England, sought her out and demanded to know why she had abandoned him. She asked him the same questions and gradually, the role played by her aunt, was discovered. James immediately offered to marry Elizabeth, but she refused. His was not the only genuine offer of marriage she refused. There were several others, one of which she was keen to accept.

As Elizabeth's liaison with the Duke of Kingston grew, he became keen to marry her. She was quite happy with this suggestion, but it meant a change of attitude towards Hervey. Now, she wanted a divorce, but without the scandal to go with it. He was happy to oblige.

As far as Pierrepont and everybody else was concerned, she was still Miss Chudleigh, and there were problems to be overcome.

The main one, which would take some thought, was the actual divorce. It was imperative Pierrepont did not know she was married. Instead of obtaining a divorce by Act of Parliament, which would have revealed her earlier marriage, she and Hervey went for a ***Jactitation Suit*** in the consistory court.

In brief she swore an oath that she had never been married and ensured no evidence to the contrary was produced. Her divorce was accepted by the Church, without a long lengthy hearing in court.

On 8 March 1769 she married Evelyn Pierrepont and became Duchess of Kingston.

He died on 23 September 1773 aged sixty-two and left her his real and personal estate albeit with a big proviso. The terms of his will only applied to her as long she never remarried. Her new-found wealth did not go down well with other members of the Duke's family. They had been looking forward to a reasonable inheritance, but instead it had all gone to his widow, about whom they knew very little.

It was time to make enquiries about her.

Elizabeth was not worried about remarrying and now fully indulged herself in an extravagant lifestyle, enjoying many lovers, reputedly of both genders and became a hardened drinker. This scandalous way of life endeared her even less to the late duke's family.

As the family, especially the duke's nephew probed more into her background, Anne Cradock, one of the witnesses to Elizabeth's secret marriage, heard about their enquiries and approached her. She offered to say nothing about the marriage, but for a price. Elizabeth offered to give her £20 (approximately £1,800 today), with the requirement she went to live in a quiet Derbyshire village. Anne refused and went to the family.

Her revelations were just what they wanted to hear.

In April 1776, Elizabeth was indicted for bigamy and chose to appear before her peers in the House of Lords. It was a sensible move on her part, as mutilation and branding were the normal punishments for anyone found guilty of bigamy in a lower court. The House of Lords did not order such barbaric punishments.

She was in Rome when the hearing was announced and resolved to return and fight the case. The problem was a shortage of funds as the duke's nephew was trying to have the will overturned, and in the meantime, the account was frozen. In the end it was not really a problem as she merely held up a friendly banker and t*ook/borrowed* what she needed.

At the hearing, the House of Lords refused to recognize the validation of the Jactitation Suit and found her guilty of bigamy. This result strengthened the nephew's hand as he contested the inheritance. The will had left the money to the duke's widow and it had just been proved, overwhelmingly, she had not been married to him. In the following lull, Elizabeth knew she had to flee the country as soon as possible.

Nevertheless, she was under no illusion of being arrested if she openly tried to leave the country. It would have to be done secretly.

Still playing a part, her coach with its coat-of-arms was driven around as if she was inside. Elizabeth also sent out numerous invitations to all manner of people for an event she was holding. They and the authorities believed her. By the time they realized the truth, Elizabeth had fled the country. As her yacht had already been seized, she was obliged to travel to France in an open boat.

Back in England, the new Earl of Bristol, Augustus Hervey, sought to have their marriage proved, as a first step towards his obtaining a divorce from her. It did not proceed very far following suggestions he had also misled the consistory court hearing. Wisely, he left the country, but was back, in London, when he died on 22 December 1779. There are suggestions he also remarried, whilst technically still married to Elizabeth. If so, he was never charged with bigamy.

Now known as the Countess of Bristol, Elizabeth spent the rest of her life living abroad. She was a big favourite of Czarina Catherine in Russia, who gave her an estate after she had already purchased one. As the years progressed, Elizabeth was described as *extremely coarse and self-indulgent*. Her least endearing habit was forever breaking wind, blaming it on any dogs or anybody else in the area. She kept company with all manner of dubious characters. Whilst she was very generous to her friends, Elizabeth was a bad enemy.

Following a court case, going against her in France, Elizabeth became so angry, she burst a blood vessel, internally, and was confined to bed. Several hours later, on 26 August 1788, at the age of sixty-eight, she got up, drank two large glasses of wine, against her doctor's orders, and went to sleep.

She never woke up.

Author's note

Was Elizabeth Hervey a wicked woman?

Perhaps she was more of a good-time girl who always kept an eye open for the main chance to better herself. For her the grass was always greener on the other side of the fence.

She was very wilful and used every charm weapon available to better herself, regardless of anybody who got in her way. It has never been established whether she robbed the banker in Rome or just persuaded him to part with the money she needed to get home.

Being unconventional came naturally and it was a way of life to her. I doubt she was alone in this manner and there were very many intrigues going on the whole time she was at court. Perhaps it was a case of if you cannot beat them, join them.

Back to the question of was Elizabeth wicked or a good time girl. There is no suggestion of her causing any real harm to anyone. In the end it all rebounded on her, yet she rose again.

I say she was not wicked, but a good time girl who took advantage of every opportunity which came her way and rose above most of them when they went wrong.

22

Ann Heytree (*circa* 1799-1820)

When Sarah Dormer engaged Ann Heytree as a domestic servant in March 1819, she never envisaged the terrible consequences of her kind intentions.

It has been suggested Ann was already a criminal, but even if that was so, Sarah felt there was some good in her and she just needed a chance. So, Ann joined Joseph, Sarah, their six children and two other servants at Dial House Farm, Ashow, between Warwick and Kenilworth.

Ann was born at Charlecote, near Wellesbourne in Warwickshire, where she received a rudimentary education. This was the village where legend has it a young William Shakespeare was caught poaching on Sir Thomas Lucy's land.

Sunday 29 August 1819 was sunny in Ashow as the Dormer family set out to enjoy the annual thanksgiving festival, known as a *Wake,* which was happening. Along with everyone else, the Dormers and their invited friends enjoyed the entertainment and a pleasant lunch.

During the early evening, everyone left the farm except Sarah Dormer and Ann Heytree. Sarah had last been seen at about 6.30pm when she gave her young nephew and niece a drink

Some of the children returned forty minutes later but were surprised and possibly a little worried to find no trace of their mother. They asked Ann where she was. Ann replied she had gone into Ashow, which she changed to her going into the garden to pick cucumbers. The children noticed how Ann seemed agitated. Then, in the hallway by the stairs, they found several drops of a red liquid and thought some wine had been spilt. But, soon afterwards, they discovered Sarah's dead body lying in her bedroom.

She had been stabbed several times in her back and hands. Lastly, Sarah's throat had been so violently cut, that her head was almost severed from her body. Clearly, the red liquid spots were her blood.

As it happened, William Boddington, a local surgeon, was riding by when he heard the children's screams. He went into the farmhouse and confirmed Sarah was dead. Suspicion fell quickly fell on to Ann, despite her denials. There was blood on her hands and under her fingernails. William immediately sealed off the room and sent for Constable Thomas Bellerby. He soon arrived, arrested Ann and took her to Warwick gaol.

When questioned about what had happened, Ann claimed Sarah had taken her own life. William Boddington quickly disproved this suggestion. He later testified in court how Sarah's wounds could not possibly have been self-inflicted. For instance, she could not have stabbed herself in the back. Just as incriminating were the defensive wounds in Sarah's hands where she had tried to defend herself.

Ann later admitted voices had told her to do it.

She was charged and later tried at Warwick Assizes for ***petty treason***, which is committed by a servant who murders his or her master or mistress: or by a wife who murders her husband

Ann had no reason to murder Sarah. She had been well treated until suddenly having this urge to kill her mistress.

The trial verdict was a forgone conclusion and she was hanged on 12 April 1820 in Barrack Street, Warwick. Part of the punishment for this crime was for the condemned to be dragged to the place of execution on a board or hurdle. Being so dragged to the gallows was all part of the punishment for high treason. There is no record of Ann having been treated this way. The gallows site immediately joined the prison, so it is unlikely this happened in her case

Following her execution. Ann's body was given to William Boddington and Warwick doctor Thomas Hiron for dissection.

Almost a year to the day, Ann's brother, Thomas, was hanged on the same gallows.

He and three others had ambushed a William Hiron in Alveston near Stratford-upon-Avon and murdered him. The dead man was Thomas Hiron's uncle.

In 1907, James Dormer of Dial House Farm, Ashow, appeared in court for shooting at Harvey Reynolds in Leek Wootton. The charge was dropped to one of assault from which he was discharged. No age is shown for James, but he was undoubtedly one of Joseph's and Sarah's descendants.

Author's comments

Was Ann Heytree wicked?

Most people would have thought so. She had murdered Sarah after being given employment by her. Looking at her case in 1819, they were probably right. But before we condemn Ann we need to ask if she was completely sane and in full control of her actions.

She had the means with the kitchen knife. Likewise, she had the opportunity in an empty house with only her and Sarah there. But where was the motive? There really was none other than she was told by the voices to kill her.

If Ann really had heard voices instructing her to kill Sarah, then she was probably suffering from auditory command hallucinations – a mental problem known about since the first century AD and is related to *schizophrenia*. Its symptoms include hearing voices instructing the sufferer to carry out acts they would not normally do. These range from the inconsequential to committing murder.

Likewise, was she responsible for her wilfulness? Was she really in control? I doubt it.

Ann clearly fell into this category, but would this have been considered in 1819? I think not.

Following an assassination attempt on George III in 1800, by John Hadfield the Criminal Lunatics Act 1800 was quickly introduced to consider the mental state of some types of criminals appearing in court. It introduced the alternative punishment of being detained during His Majesty's Pleasure as an alternative to hanging. The problem was they first had to be found guilty before being so detained.

Being classed as unfit to plead did not appear until 1964.

Had it been available in 1820, then Ann should have been classed as unfit to plead, as hopefully she would have been treated two hundred years later. Alternatively, she could still have been tried and convicted, but detained during His Majesty's Pleasure.

There had been an earlier precedent for such action at Warwick Assizes in 1812.

In this instance, a young servant girl had been shot dead for no apparent reason. The perpetrator was a retired vicar, referred as 'Mad Brookes' and was clearly mentally ill. Unlike Ann, who had no one to defend her in court, his family had influence, hence him not being hanged.

It was very much a law for the influential and another for everybody else.

23

Marion Humphris (?-1892-?)

For a young girl with very few, if any prospects, when Rachel Slate was offered the position of being a domestic servant, it was too good an opportunity to miss. As an orphan from London, it meant travelling to the North Warwickshire village of Warton, not far from Atherstone and close to the Leicestershire border.

She had been offered the post by a middle-aged man who was seeking a servant for his married daughter, Marion Humphris. Living in a ten roomed house, Marion was not poor, and her father had undertaken to find a servant for his daughter. Rachel was in her early teens and having been in service before, readily accepted the offer. It came with an annual salary of £9 (approximately £1,000 today) plus three meals a day, lodging, and time off to go to church.

She travelled to Atherstone with Marion's father by train and completed the journey by *dogcart*. In due course she arrived at Warton and met her new mistress. All too soon Rachel realized this was not going to be the job of her dreams: more correctly the job of her nightmares.

It was only on arriving at the house Rachel discovered how, she and the cook were the only domestic servants for this large house. And if this was not bad enough, worse was to follow.

In addition to all her housework, Rachel also had to look after Marion's new baby. Rachel was told how giving birth had exhausted her so much, she was unable to tend to the child's needs. Despite these extra duties, Rachel set to with a will and tried her best. Very long and tiring days followed with no let up.

There was not the slightest chance of her getting to church as she was too busy. Likewise, despite the promises, there were no proper meals for her. Just very occasionally there might be, but these were very rare. Rachel was instructed to '*grab some crusts as you pass through the kitchen*.'

Rachel had to bathe the baby, supervised by Marion, who always tested the water first. If it was too hot, Rachel was in trouble and if too cold, more trouble followed.

On a good day, Rachel might get to bed at about 3.00am if she was lucky, only to be up two or three hours later.

Towards the end of April, Marion complained about Rachel not cleaning the house properly and ordered her upstairs and take off her clothes. Here she beat the poor girl with a silver topped cane which Rachel described later as being '*as thick as a thumb*.' Another similar beating followed. A week later, Rachel was in trouble again and ordered upstairs, but this time she refused, not that it did any her good. Marion threatened her with even worse punishments, so Rachel submitted to a further beating.

On 7 June, Rachel was beaten again because the baby's bath water was not hot enough. Her employer used the same stick, but did not wait for her to go upstairs, immediately beating the poor girl about the face and breasts. When Marion had finished, she gave Rachel a slice of dry toast to eat. There was no food at all next day, and the provisions had been locked away to stop her helping herself. Marion beat Rachel again and threatened her with more. It was the last straw for Rachel, who was absolutely exhausted both mentally and physically and knew she had to get away from this terrible house.

She waited until Marion and her husband were having their evening meal and then slipped out and hid in the garden. Fortunately, it was a short, warm summery night, and she did not have too long to wait before dawn broke. Doubtless it would have seemed like an endless night to Rachel.

When it was light enough to see Rachel left the garden and walked into Warton. She did not have the faintest idea of where she needed to go, provided it was far away from that hateful house. It was a challenge especially as she had only been out of the house just twice since her arrival.

Now Rachel had a stroke of luck as the first person she met was Emma

Stuffins.

It only took Emma a few seconds to realize the girl was obviously in great distress. Taking Rachel by the hand, she took her straight to where Police Constable Harby Ford lived. He was the village constable but was out when they arrived. His wife quickly took charge and gave Rachel some food, but the girl could not keep it down. Meanwhile, she had directed Emma where to find her husband.

When Harby arrived, he saw the girl was ill. The marks on her face where Marion had beaten her were obvious, so were the bruises on her shoulders, and it did not take an expert to see she had been badly treated. He described her later as being *depressed and ill.*

The following month, Marion appeared at Warwick Quarter Sessions charged with assaulting Rachel.

There was great interest shown in the case as it came at a time when the **National Society for the Prevention of Cruelty to Children** was in its infancy. It defies belief how some critics of the new society, blamed it for resulting in Marion's prosecution. No one was surprised when she pleaded not guilty to the charge. Her obvious intention was to create a favourable impression from the outset. Not for her was the role of a shrinking violet.

Her attitude throughout was one of indignation.

She wore a short pale green costume, black jacket and bonnet with grey feathers which *well suited her forty-five years.* The court was left in no doubt about her important social standing in Warwickshire society. Quickly seeing through her ploy, the Crown carefully pointed out to the jury how it was the facts of the case which mattered: not her social standing.

Rachel delivered her evidence in a quiet and subdued manner as she related her experiences at the hands of Marion Humphris. She had not been paid but when she complained to Mr Humphris, he replied *it is none of my business.* He denied having heard her scream and being present when one of the beatings took place.

She stood her ground resolutely whilst being cross-examined, especially when it was suggested Marion had been ill since Christmas with a heart complaint.

'She could still use the stick well enough!' Rachel replied stoutly, much to

the amusement of people in court.

Dr William Smith testified to examining Rachel on behalf of the police. He described the bruises found on her buttocks, arms, shoulders, left breast and eyebrow. It was his opinion, shared with Harby Ford, that Rachel had been severely beaten on more than one occasion.

Written defence evidence was submitted from Dr de Caux, who said the marks on Rachel's body were not bruises from a beating, but as a result of the **arsenica** which alleged had been used to treat her **eczema**. These views were ridiculed by the Crown. No reason was shown as to why he did not appear in person to give this evidence. Could it have been because he knew the Crown would tear it to shreds?

Marion's father testified to having clothed Rachel at his own expense, along with her rail fare. It is fair to say the court was not particularly impressed and fell about laughing when he described his daughter's kindness. He considered her to be totally incapable of striking a horse, dog or any other animal, let alone a servant girl.

His opinions were fully supported by her father-in-law and other employees.

In his summing up, her barrister concentrated on the eczema treatment. He ended by reinforcing his client's standing in society. Rachel might possibly have been lazy, but he added it was possible she just could not do the work in the available time. But he said forcefully, even if she was lazy, he could not see his client acting in such a way.

After sitting through several hours of evidence, the jury made a token retirement before finding Marion guilty. Before he imposed a sentence, the judge called for medical evidence about her health.

At this point, who should arrive to give such evidence, but Dr de Caux: the same person who had stated Rachel's bruises were not caused by a beating, but by eczema treatment. He agreed Marion was in a weak state but had not found any evidence of heart trouble.

Protesting to the end, Marion Humphris was sentenced to the very apt punishment of three months in prison with hard labour.

Her father called out: *'Oh! Monstrous! Monstrous!'* But no one listened to him.

Throughout this sorry tale, Mr Humphis has been deliberately kept very much in the background. His correct title was: The Reverend Mr Humphris.

Marion Humphris was the wife of the vicar of Holy Trinity Church at Warton.

Author's comments

Was Marion Humphris a wicked woman?

Although this case occurred in 1892, it was still very much a law for the rich and another for the poor. This trial attracted a great deal of media and social reformers interest. Marion was firmly of the old school whereby her position in society was what really mattered, never mind the welfare of her staff. Despite all the above, she failed to impress the jury and was punished accordingly.

I am still at a loss to understand her husband's role in all this, especially as a cleric who should be dedicated to looking after the poor and needy as well as encouraging his staff to go to church. Was he completely under Marion's thumb, because I fail to believe he did not know what she was doing? Or was it possibly more of a Pontius Pilate's action of washing his hands of the matter and leaving it to Marion?

Rachel had a lucky escape. Clearly the vicar and his wife were unaware she had gone, or did they not care? What would have happened if Rachel had not met Emma Stuffins?

The other unanswered questions are what happened to Rachel's predecessor? Had she also been ill-treated? Why was there only one domestic servant to clean and look after a ten roomed house? I suspect no locals would work for Marion as they knew only too well how she ill-treated her staff.

Despite her being part of Warwickshire's society, I would argue her behaviour was certainly unconventional even amongst her peers.

I think Marion Humphris was a wicked and wilful woman, unless she was being affected by an underlying medical condition. Possibly this might have been brought on by the effects of giving birth, which had disturbed the balance of her mind. Hopefully her unconventional behavior was not typical of other employers in the Warton area.

24
Sarah Kibler (?-1889-?)

Poison is a well-recognized weapon used by women for a variety of reasons such as financial gain, and this was the case with Sarah Kibler.

Early in February 1889, Elizabeth Horniblow from Leamington Spa, Warwickshire, was taken quite ill with a sudden paralysis. Her husband, Dr William Horniblow, was unable to nurse her, care for their fourteen years old son, also called William, the house and his medical practice.

He desperately needed some help.

Before the month was out, he had employed Sarah Kibler as housekeeper both for the house and his surgery. This enabled him to spend more time with Elizabeth, who slowly started to recover.

Sarah quickly took to running the house and surgery with great efficiency. Although her new employer was relieved to see the improvement in his wife's health, Sarah was not. She had quickly settled in and could see a good long-term future ahead of her. Her new position was well paid and came with other material benefits such as food and accommodation. An improvement in Elizabeth's health was the last thing she wanted, believing, correctly, it would number the days in her new and very comfortable situation.

She now tasked herself with finding some means to prolong her employment, hopefully making it permanent. But to do this, she needed to get rid of Elizabeth permanently. As her duties included cleaning the surgery, Sarah was well aware of the various medicines and poisons which were kept there. One such chemical was *corrosive sublimate*, which she knew was a powerful poison.

This was how Sarah intended to murder her mistress.

Before administering any doses, she started setting the scene by callously spreading rumours about Elizabeth's health deteriorating to such a degree, adding there was little chance of her surviving. By 7 March she set about the next and most important stage of her plan: administering the poison to Elizabeth.

On that afternoon, Sarah could not believe her luck when Elizabeth asked for a cup of tea. She was more than happy to provide it and added some corrosive sublimate at the same time. With a thumping heart, Sarah handed the tea to her mistress and watched her swallow the first mouthful. What happened next was most spectacular and certainly not what Sarah had expected nor wanted.

Elizabeth immediately spat it out complaining how it tasted of copper and sulphur. Moments later she was violently sick which probably saved her life. She would, however, complain about her mouth and throat burning. But as the symptoms passed, the incident was forgotten, but not by Sarah.

A few days later, Sarah, saw the milkman, Joseph Bellamy, and confided in him how Elizabeth would never recover. Once she had his attention, Sarah said she had heard a man's unexplained footsteps on the landing. She gravely explained this was a sign of an impending death in the household. Joseph was suitably upset by this tale as he liked the Horniblow family. No doubt he passed the gossip on to his other customers, just as Sarah meant him to do. It is easy to imagine his surprise a few days later, when he saw Elizabeth looking in the best of health.

Nevertheless, just four days later there was a death in the house.

Elizabeth's pet rat died suddenly with a very swollen body. Sarah was delighted with the rodent's death for two reasons. Firstly, she detested it and secondly her poisoning experiment on the animal had worked. Now all she needed was something to disguise the taste of the poison. Elizabeth was too upset by the creature's death to clear away its cage and Sarah declined to do it, which would prove to be a big mistake.

The rat still had an important role to play.

Meanwhile, Elizabeth's health continued improving and Sarah realized her days in the house were numbered. She needed to act quickly before it was too late.

Her chance came when she saw Elizabeth mix herself a brandy and water in a cup. Then leaving it untouched on the table, she went into the garden with her son. It was the moment Sarah had been waiting for.

Wasting no time, she quickly added some corrosive sublimate to the brandy and waited impatiently for Elizabeth to return.

She returned at last and took a sip from the cup. Once again, she spat it out complaining of the taste and threw the cup down with such force it broke. Sarah knew she had failed, and her employment ended soon afterwards. Deep down Sarah must have realized how she was lucky, not to have been found out.

She had totally forgotten about the rat, but unbeknown to her, the creature was about to have its revenge.

By now Elizabeth felt strong enough to dispose of the rat's cage, although she could not do it herself, so her husband agreed to do it for her. Whilst removing its little rug, he saw some strange crystals on the cage's floor, which were later revealed to be corrosive sublimate. He called the family together and they remembered how Sarah had tended to the rat during Elizabeth's illness. Any lingering doubts any of them might have had, disappeared when the broken brandy cup was recovered and also found to contain crystals of corrosive sublimate.

Dr Horniblow went to the magistrates to lay evidence against Sarah. He was dismayed when they refused to accept his evidence, because it was not given under oath, but had been affirmed instead. Undeterred, he conducted his own investigation. An independent analysis of the crystals confirmed they were indeed corrosive sublimate. A subsequent confrontation between them was less productive. It ended with William referring to Sarah as 'a .... old hag.' His actual words were not reported.

Armed with the professional analysis evidence of the poison, the magistrates now acted, and Sarah appeared at Warwick Assizes in December, where she pleaded not guilty to attempted murder. It was a serious matter but not without some humorous moments. Sarah's barrister kept referring to Dr Horniblow as Dr Hornblower and had to be corrected each time amidst much laughter.

It was stressed in the hearing how the Birmingham City analyst found thirty grains of corrosive sublimate in the brandy cup. As just three grains would cause death, Elizabeth was very fortunate.

The jury made a token retirement of just fifteen minutes before returning a guilty verdict, Sarah, still protesting her innocence was sentenced to fifteen years penal servitude. As she was led away, Sarah turned to Dr Horniblow and warned him darkly how he would *'have to answer on his death bed.'*

Before the court rose, the judge soundly criticized the Leamington magistrates for failing to act on Dr Horniblow's first complaint.

Author's comments

Sarah Kibler was unconventional, but was she a wicked woman?

She had the motive of wanting permanent employment. The means was using the corrosive sublimate which was very easy for her to obtain from the surgery. Two opportunities presented themselves, both of which she took. Poisoning is a pre-meditated crime. Luckily Elizabeth spat it out on both occasions.

Sarah might have known about the poisonous effects of corrosive sublimate, but fortunately had little idea of the quantity to use or its distinctive evil taste. Clearly, she had no real plans of what to do once Elizabeth had taken the fatal dose.

It never occurred to her to remove the rat's cage. Had she done so and the broken cup, no one would have been any the wiser. Her limited knowledge did not extend as far as what sort of residue the poison would leave. Possibly she based all her actions on seeing the container was marked poison and decided to use it. For someone who was prepared to commit murder, fortunately she was incredibly squeamish when it came to the rat.

Did it not occur to her if she succeeded in murdering Elizabeth that would not be the end of the matter? If someone dies unexpectedly for no apparent reason, especially in a doctor's house, there would almost be a post-mortem. In that event, it would not have taken long to discover signs of the poisoning. Clearly, Sarah would not have wanted her employer to take the blame, because if he was hanged, she would lose her job. The only other possibility would have been suicide, which in the absence of any note might just have aroused some suspicions about her death being one of murder. Although such notes are common, the lack of one does not rule out suicide.

As so often happens, murderers and would-be murderers, such as Sarah Kibler are discovered following their making stupid mistakes.

I have little doubt Sarah Kibler was guilty as charged. Luckily for her, attempted murder ceased to be a capital offence in 1861.

As affirming in court is an acceptable way of testifying, I cannot understand the magistrates' reluctance to accept Dr Horniblow's complaint. The judge's criticism was well justified. Had the magistrates rejected the first analysis of the poison as not being carried out independently, they would have had a stronger case. But why did Dr Horniblow not go to the police or why did the magistrates not direct him there in the first place if they wanted to get rid of him and his problem.?

To sum up, I consider Sarah Kibler to be both wicked and wilful, albeit in a somewhat limited way. She was also unconventional in trying to murder her mistress.

25

Mary Mallon *aka* Mary Brown and Typhoid Mary (1869-1938)

Mary's case is completely different to any of the others in this book.

She was born in at Cookstown, County Tyrone, but migrated to the United States of America in 1883 and lived with relatives for a while in New York. In time she was employed as a cook for wealthy families, which turned out to be a grave and fatal mistake.

Between 1900 and 1907, she worked for seven different families.

Within two weeks of her starting with the first family, the residents developed *typhoid* fever. After moving in 1901 to another employer, members and servants of that family contracted various fevers and diarrhoea, one of whom, the laundress, died. It was a similar same story when she moved on to other employers.

Soon after she started a new employment, members of the families became ill.

Between 27 August and 3 September 1906, she worked for Charles Henry Warren, a wealthy New York banker, who hired a house in Oyster Bay for the summer. During these few days, six members of his family were diagnosed with having typhoid fever. The doctors who treated them were concerned. Oyster Bay was normally typhoid free. But, despite their concerns, nothing further seems to have been done.

Meanwhile, Mary was hired by other families, and more outbreaks of typhoid fever followed her.

One of her new employers was so concerned about these outbreaks, he hired typhoid researcher George Soper, to make some enquiries and try to discover what had happened.

His initial investigations discovered how the outbreak began some three weeks after the family engaged a new cook, known as Mary Mallon. She did not stay long and moved on soon after the outbreak started. Mary was described as '*Irish, aged about forty, well-built, and apparently in good health.*' It did not take Soper long to connect her with the other outbreaks where she had worked. She normally left her employment soon after an outbreak began and without leaving a forwarding address.

Then he heard of another outbreak of typhoid in Park Avenue where the cook was called Mary Mallon. Two of the servants were put into hospital and the family's daughter died. Soper wasted no time and went to interview her, but Mary was not at all helpful.

He outlined his belief she could be an unwitting carrier of the disease and added there was a simple test which would give him the answer. All he wanted was sample of her urine and faeces. Mary was adamant the outbreaks were nothing to do with her and she refused to provide him with the samples.

Despite this setback, Soper would not be defeated. Faced with all the known facts to date, he began compiling a record of her employment. It made for scary reading, but also confirmed his worst fears.

Mallon had been employed as a cook for eight families, seven of whom claimed they had contracted typhoid whilst she was there. To be fair to Soper, he was not looking for a scapegoat, but genuinely wanted to find the source of this disease.

In the first few years of the twentieth century great progress had been made regarding the causes of typhoid. So why was it now recurring amongst wealthy New York families, especially where a Mary Mallon had been their cook at the time?

Soper reasoned Mary Mallon had to be the cause.

Knowing she had refused to see Soper and another doctor, the New York

City Health Department now sent one of their physicians to see her. They were worried by Soper's discoveries. Mallon remained uncooperative and maintained she had done nothing wrong and the law was persecuting her. The Health Department disagreed and a few days later, she was arrested, but only after quite a struggle, aggravated by Mary defending herself with a large carving fork.

Two things happened whilst she was in prison.

Firstly, she had to give samples of urine and faeces, which confirmed Mary was a carrier with the bacteria almost certainly residing in her gall bladder. Secondly, the media now christened her *'Typhoid Mary'*.

She admitted not seeing any need to wash her hands before handling food, maintaining not doing so did not pose any risk. Likewise, she was not prepared to give up working as a cook and neither would she consent to having her gall bladder removed. As far as Mallon was concerned, she refused to believe she carried the disease and remained in denial.

It was a stalemate, but the Health Department had another card to play.

Under the provisions of sections 1169 and 1170 of the Greater New York Charter, she was held in isolation at a clinic on North Brother Island.

In 1910, the New York State Commissioner of Health decided disease carriers should not be kept in isolation. He was happy for Mallon to be released, provided she agreed to stop working as a cook and took reasonable precautions to avoid spreading typhoid to other people. Mallon agreed to stop working as a cook and to take hygienic precautions to protect anyone she had contact with.

This was all set out in an affidavit and after agreeing to these terms, she was released.

After working as a laundress for a while, Mallon missed the better salaried position of a cook, so she changed her name to Mary Brown and was soon back working with food, despite having been expressly forbidden to so.

In 1915 Mallon was working at the Sloane Hospital for Women in New York where she caused another outbreak of typhoid. Twenty-five people were infected, two of whom died. Not waiting to see what happened, she disappeared, but not for long. Her arrest soon followed, and she returned to isolation on North Brother Island. Still refusing to accept she was a carrier, Mallon declined to have her gall bladder removed.

Mallon remained here until she died in 1938 from **pneumonia**. But she had been suffering from paralysis following a stroke in 1932. A post-mortem examination confirmed what had always been suspected. Typhoid bacteria, *salmonella typhi* was found in her gall bladder.

Her body was cremated.

Author's comments

Was Mary Mallon a wicked woman?

This is not an easy case to answer. She was an unwitting carrier of typhoid, at least in her early days. We shall never know at what stage she must have realized something was not right. The question is when did she realize? Before or after she first went into detention? Is her refusal to acknowledge it, the same as realizing?

If we agree she was originally an innocent carrier, can we really excuse her for agreeing not to practice as a cook anymore and then going ahead and doing so? I would argue changing her name in these circumstances indicates guilty knowledge. Right from her first contact with George Soper, she remained un-cooperative, and vehemently denied any connection between the typhoid outbreaks and her cooking. Mary always insisted she was healthy.

It is believed she was responsible for the deaths of at least three people, but her continual moving jobs and possible use of aliases makes it impossible to be completely accurate. Some estimates put the total deaths at her door of more like fifty rather than three.

What also bothers me is the question of references. Was she never asked to provide any? What would they have shown? Another possibility is she started on a trial until they arrived. Then when they did, she left or went just before their arrival, without leaving a forwarding address. There is no suggestion she forged them, but then there is much we do not know about her.

Mallon was the first *asymptomatic carrier* to be identified and there were no guidelines for handling her situation. With all her denials and refusing to have her gall bladder removed, the authorities had no alternative. She had to be kept in permanent quarantine.

Another question is where did she learn to cook? Was she taught by someone or was it something Mary picked up herself? I would have thought hygiene formed part of any cookery course had she been taught by someone. But as hygiene did not figure in her vocabulary, I am inclined to think she was self-taught.

I can accept Mallon had no say in becoming a carrier, but her persistence in carrying on cooking despite agreeing not to do so, is an act of selfishness and would justify her being called wicked and very wilful. If not unconventional, Mary Mallon's case is unusual

Ironically, her infamy lives on as all subsequent typhoid carriers are known as 'Typhoid Mary'.

26

Maria Manning *née* de (le) Roux (1821-1849) and Frederick George Manning (?-1849)

Although dealt with as husband and wife, Maria was the driving force behind this sordid affair, sometimes referred to as *The Bermondsey Horror.*

She was born Maria or Marie de Roux or le Roux in Lausanne, Switzerland. In time she emigrated to Britain and became a personal maid to Lady Blantyre, daughter of the Duchess of Sutherland. This employment gave her an insatiable taste for luxurious living, fueled by the elegant surroundings where she worked. Whilst Maria might have had some idea about poverty, living amongst such opulence decided her there was no way she would ever become poor no matter what it took.

Money was the big and only goal in her life.

Whilst on a cross Channel boat to Boulogne with Lady Blantyre, she first met Patrick O'Connor, a middle-aged Irishman, who worked as a customs officer in London. But, much more to the point, he enjoyed a reasonably substantial private income. In other words, Patrick was wealthy which made him immediately attractive to Maria.

However, she was also seeing Frederick George Manning, who worked as a guard on the Great Western Railway, which was not so very well paid. The matter was further complicated by the fact both men had proposed to her.

Which one should she choose?

Manning was nearer her own age and a much weaker character. On the other hand, whilst Patrick was older and a heavy drinker, he had money. In the end she married Manning in 1847, but she was not yet finished with O'Connor.

The newly-weds had enough money between them to afford a stylish home, 3 Minver Place, situated in Bermondsey. Manning possibly supplemented his meagre salary by thieving. One thing is certain, they needed money to run such a house.

By August 1849, Maria was ready with her plan to get hold of Patrick's wealth.

On 8 August she invited him to dinner, having already briefed her husband and acquired a shovel and a quantity of *quicklime*. She had also prepared a grave for Patrick in the kitchen.

Possibly Patrick was suspicious, as he duly arrived for his dinner date bringing a friend with him. Undeterred, Maria persuaded him to come again the following evening, but this time to be alone. He did so, believing her suggestion how they might be more intimate just on their own.

On Patrick's arrival, she suggested he might want to wash his hands and led him out to the sink. As he stood there, with his back turned to her, she shot him in the head, but failed to kill him. So, her husband completed the job with a crowbar, known as a ripping chisel. They buried Patrick in the kitchen grave after first covering him in quicklime to speed up the body's decaying. Having carefully replaced the slabs over him, they cemented them into place.

During the next two days, Maria carefully ransacked Patrick's lodgings and removed anything of value, including his share certificates. Then two days later, everything started to go wrong when the Mannings received a visit.

The two men introduced themselves as being Patrick's colleagues, who had apparently disappeared, and Minver Place was believed to be his last known siting on the 9th. Maria and Frederick admitted he had dined with them on the previous day but denied having seen him since. The men departed but left behind a thoroughly worried Maria and Frederick.

They believed, albeit erroneously, these men were police officers. They panicked and decided to leave London as soon as possible.

Maria tasked Frederick the next day with selling all their furniture. Once he had left the house, she packed up everything of value, and going to Kings Cross railway station caught a train to Edinburgh. Frederick probably had no idea where she had gone. Nevertheless, he decided it would be a good idea to leave the country and sailed to Jersey.

Meanwhile, Patrick's colleagues had reported his disappearance to the police, including their suspicions about the Mannings.

The police wasted no time in making a thorough search of Minver Place. They noticed in the kitchen, how the mortar between two of the flagstones was damp. A few minutes later the flagstones had been lifted and Patrick's bloodied body was found, and a murder hunt began.

The cabbie who had taken her to Kings Cross came forward. He told the police how they had stopped at another station first and deposited two trunks. It did not take long to discover she had travelled to Scotland and the Edinburgh police were informed.

Maria, however, was already in custody.

She had tried to sell some of Patrick's railway shares to an Edinburgh stockbroker, who was suspicious of her French accent. Believing them to have been stolen and wary about becoming a fraud victim, he called the police.

Maria was soon back in London, charged with Patrick's murder and lodged in the Horsemonger Lane Gaol. Her husband did not remain at liberty for much longer.

He had been recognized in Jersey by a man who knew him and was aware of his being wanted for murder. On returning to London, he informed the police. Sergeant Langley went to Jersey where he arrested Frederick.

Once in custody, Frederick admitted Maria had shot Patrick whilst he had '...*battered his head with a ripping chisel.*' He too was soon lodged in Horsemonger Lane Gaol.

Their trial began on 25 October at the Old Bailey and lasted for two days. Apparently, they had each expected the other to accept responsibility for the murder: but neither would. The jury took less than an hour to find them both guilty. At this point, Maria lost her composure. She screamed at the jury and raved at the judge: not that it made any difference.

Whilst in the condemned cell, Maria wrote to Lady Blantyre and Queen Victoria asking for them to intercede on her behalf and issue a reprieve. Queen Victoria had taken an interest in the case, but considered the verdict was the correct one. Maria had also written to Frederick asking him to accept full responsibility for the murder. He might have been a weak character, but he was not completely stupid and ignored her plea.

Their executions took place on Tuesday 13th November at the prison where they were held. It was believed the crowd was 30-50,000 strong and every available viewing point was taken. William Calcraft was the hangman and made some money selling off locks of her hair as souvenirs. No doubt he would have cut the noose up into strips and sold those as well. Hence the expression 'Money for old rope.' Maria quickly made it into Madame Tussaud's Chamber of Horrors, where her effigy and actual dress were soon on show, probably supplied by Calcraft. Undoubtedly there would have been an artist in court to copy her likeness.

Ironically, when their bodies were buried later that day, they were both covered in quicklime.

Charles Dickens was amongst the spectators, although he was a staunch supporter of the abolishment of public executions. Undoubtedly, he used Maria as his role model for Mademoiselle Hortense, who was Lady Dedlock's maid in *Bleak House*. He described her as being '*like a tamed she-wolf,*' which could definitely apply to Maria.

Author's comments

I cannot think anyone would disagree Maria was wicked, wilful, unconventional and is best described as a thoroughly nasty piece of work. A woman who was driven solely by greed.

Her motive was robbery: the means shooting and clubbing: and the opportunity when the victim was a guest in her house, where he should have been able to trust his hosts, not be murdered by them.

Interestingly she failed to kill him, and it was left to Frederick to finish the work. Technically, she did not kill him outright, but we shall never know if Patrick might have died later. In her true evil fashion, she tried to shift the blame for the actual death on to her husband. Not that it would have made much difference. At the very least she would have faced a charge of attempted murder, which was still a capital offence until 1861. Perhaps Maria was trying to shift the full blame on to Frederick, maintaining she had been forced into the crime.

Whichever way we look at it, this was a pre-meditated and pre-planned crime involving the pair of them.

As can well be imagined, this crime attracted a tremendous amount of public interest. It was a classic case of murder, robbery and sexual intrigue, which made for a great public scandal. For the shocked Victorians there was only one redeeming factor. Maria was of Swiss origin and therefore she was not English.

The Nation's morals remained unsullied!

27
Florence Elizabeth Maybrick
née Chandler (1862-1941)

Whilst travelling to England in 1881, Caroline Chandler and her daughter Florence met James Maybrick. They were all on board a White Star liner, and for Florence and James it was love at first sight. They believed he was a successful cotton broker, albeit twenty-three years older than Florence. Much to the amusement or scandal of the other passengers, they were rarely seen apart.

On 27 July 1881, Florence Elizabeth Chandler (19), married James Maybrick (42), in London. James Maybrick's sudden marriage caused a few upsets back in his home city of Liverpool.

For instance, Matilda Briggs, née Janion, previously engaged to James, was now separated from her husband. There can be little doubt she intended to resume their earlier relationship and firmly believed marriage to James was now a distinct possibility. And she was not the only one. There was another woman, by whom he already had three children. Some mystery surrounds her identity, but she might have been Gertrude Janion who was Matilda's sister. Or, she might have been Sarah Robertson, who later referred to herself as Sarah Maybrick, claiming to have been secretly married to James.

As Florence soon discovered, James was a **hypochondriac**, always concerned about his health, especially his stomach. Consequently, he was regularly seen by the doctor and prescribed various medicines. These were in addition to the patent ones he purchased himself. Not convinced about the effectiveness of the prescribed dosages, James allegedly always doubled them. Many of these patent or quack medicines contained *arsenic* and *strychnine*.

In fairness to James, he had contracted *malaria* in the past and took arsenic, or so he said, to prevent any recurrences. Consuming arsenic was also a recognized sexual stimulant in the days long before *Viagra*. If the comments about him having another wife and mistresses are true, then his needing such a stimulant is highly possible.

To all outward appearances, they made an ideal couple. An attractive woman, from the Southern States of America, she fitted the role of a successful man's wife, by being an excellent hostess. Whilst many people envied them, their relationship was not quite so simple, or enviable.

Despite his earlier boasting, James was not as successful as he liked everyone to believe, and money was in short supply. Possibly he might have married Florence in the expectation of acquiring her family's wealth, but two things spoiled those plans.

Firstly, she was not as wealthy as everyone had thought. Secondly, the passing of the *Married Women's Property Acts* in 1870 and 1882 established the right of a wife to do what she wished with her own property. It no longer automatically belonged to her husband.

By 1888, the couple and their two children, plus several servants, lived at Battlecrease House, Aigburth, Liverpool. Florence was well aware their financial affairs were in a poor way, as he continually kept cutting her housekeeping allowance. It was about now when Florence discovered her husband's secret affairs.

She was not prepared to meekly accept he had a mistress, let alone the reports of him having several, and was something of a serial womanizer. Another unconfirmed report suggested he had since fathered another two children on his secret wife.

James had now grown cold and indifferent to Florence, which with all the other problems, put their marriage under a considerable strain. To make matters worse, James was undergoing a period of health problems and taking several medicines which contained strychnine. She told this to her doctor, who promised to bear it in mind should anything happen to her husband.

If James thought Florence would meekly accept him continuing his affairs after they were married, he was sadly mistaken. This betrayal, along with their financial problems, made Florence start looking for other male company.

She was believed to be close to Edwin Maybrick, one of James's brothers. However, there is no real evidence to support they were anything more than just good friends. But later the same year, she first met Alfred Brierley, another cotton broker.

He had lived some time in Alabama and was the opposite of James in just about every way from business success to physical appearance and charm. For the next few months, he was adamant they only met in the company of other people, but matters changed on 21 March 1889, when they left for a secret weekend together in London.

Florence had booked them into Flatman's Hotel, off Cavendish Square, London, in the names of Mr & Mrs Maybrick. James believed she had gone to visit an aunt. Whilst the lovers only spent two days together, Florence did not return just yet, as she began planning to divorce James. In fact, these plans were later dropped. Having used the same hotel, as many of James's business colleagues, she must have known it would only be a matter of time before he heard about her stay there with Alfred. Possibly that was her intention.

Once again, reports differ on what happened next. One source recorded James knew nothing about their visit, but others disagree. It also seems Alfred, whilst not minding the weekend fling did not wish for such a permanent arrangement with her. Initially, it seemed Florence accepted that arrangement.

Or did she?

On 29 March 1889, only a few days after her return from London, she and James went to Aintree, for the races. Who should be there, but Alfred Brierley! Florence flirted with him in front of James, which was not well received. Taking Alfred by the arm, they went to see the Prince of Wales, who was also there. On their return some reports stated how James and Florence quarreled on the racecourse, much to the amusement of the spectators. Another version maintained they waited until they got home before having the quarrel. A third story maintains both events happened.

Whatever happened, James did not enjoy being made to look stupid and they had a violent argument at some stage, in which Florence received a black eye and she threatened to leave him. James warned if she did then Battlecrease House would be closed to her. This meant she would never see her children again. As moving in with Alfred was not an option, she stayed with James.

For the next few days, there was an uneasy truce between the couple and matters began to return to what passed for normal. Later research suggests this was when Florence began purchasing fly papers. These contained arsenic and were freely available in the shops. Initially she had said there was a problem with flies at their house, but later admitted they were for cosmetic reasons.

On 13 April, James went to visit his brother, Michael, in London, but was taken ill on his arrival. He complained of pains in the head and a numbness in his right leg. Michael's doctor examined James but found nothing drastically wrong with him. He recovered sufficiently and returned to Liverpool nine days later.

James was taken ill again on 27 April, with severe vomiting, after having taken a dose of *nux vomica*, which basically was strychnine. James went to work and dined in the evening with friends. There he had a fit of violent trembling and spilled his wine. The next day he complained about a general feeling of paralysis in the region of his heart and chest. A doctor diagnosed *dyspepsia* aggravated by some bad brandy. Edwin was informed and he came straight away to Battlecrease House, to supervise its running until James recovered.

Two days later, Florence purchased some skin lotion and more flypapers. Meanwhile, James returned to work. But, by now, the servants were all talking about his illness and Florence having been seen soaking the flypapers, to remove the arsenic. She always maintained this had to be done, before it could be used on her skin.

As the month ended, James was given some beef tea, made by the cook and handed over to him by Florence. James actively disliked beef tea, complaining it made him feel nauseous. The next day, he was ill again and coming home from his office took to his bed. Once again, the doctor was called, but he could find nothing drastically wrong with him. After he had gone, Nurse Alice Yapp (28), the family nursemaid, chosen for the job by James, without involving Florence, suggested a second medical opinion was needed although Florence disagreed.

By 4 May, James had worsened and being unable to keep any food down, stayed in bed. Yet again, the doctor was unable to diagnose what was wrong, although he suggested all the medical overdosing James was doing was to blame.

On 7 May, a second medical opinion was sought.

The new doctor diagnosed dyspepsia and acute inflammation of the stomach. Later that day Nurse Yapp saw Florence combining the contents of two medicine bottles. She told Matilda Briggs what she had seen and voiced her suspicions about what was happening. Matilda immediately sent for Michael Maybrick to come from London. Meanwhile Edwin Maybrick arranged for private nurses to attend his brother.

That afternoon, Florence instructed Nurse Alice Yapp to take her daughter Gladys to post a letter.

What happened next, was according to Nurse Yapp's testimony in court.

Florence handed over a letter which did not take her long to see was addressed to Alfred Brierley. She gave the letter to Gladys to post. Although the recent rain had stopped, it was still wet under foot. Happily skipping along the road, Gladys dropped the letter into a puddle. Nurse Yapp considered the envelope was too wet to use and as she transferred it into a fresh one, started to read it.

The first word was *Dearest*!

Nurse Yapp maintained this was the first she knew about Florence's affair, which may or may not be true. She related how shocked she was and seriously thought there was something more sinister behind James's illness and Florence was its cause. Hurrying back to the house, she handed the letter to Edwin and Matilda Briggs. She knew the staff also thought James was being poisoned.

The letter, according to Florence, was a clear indication James had not known about their weekend in London. Alfred had worried about the truth coming out and was contemplating leaving the country. Florence begged him not to, at least not until she had seen him again.

In the letter Florence used phrases such as *dearest....my darling....my own darling...* words which would damn her, morally at least, in the eyes of polite Victorian society, regardless of how hypocritical they were. According to Alice Yapp, these were some of the words she accidentally saw, and felt obliged to read on. It was what compelled her to give the letter to the others.

Although Edwin and Florence had always enjoyed a good relationship, he could not ignore the comments in the letter coupled with the sudden sinister suspicions about his brother's illness.

Believing James might have been poisoned, numerous tests took place on samples of his body waste, but they revealed no traces of any arsenic or any other poisons. In fact, if anything, the results served only to confirm the original diagnosis of severe food poisoning. Nevertheless, all the brothers, who were now at the house, agreed only the nurses should tend James, although Florence could still visit him. Understandably, this decision offended her.

On 10 May, Michael also saw Florence transferring part of the contents from one medicine bottle to another. Florence explained she was merely condensing the two, as the sediment in the smaller bottle made it hard to shake. The medicine was tested, but no traces of arsenic were found, which confirmed her story.

During the afternoon, one of the nurses witnessed the following conversation, between James and his wife:

'*You have given me the wrong medicine again,*' said James.

'*What are you talking about? You never had the wrong medicine,*' Florence replied.

Later that evening, another nurse heard the following conversation between them.

'*Oh Bunny, Bunny, how could you do it? I did not think it of you,*' asked James. He repeated it. Bunny was his pet name for her.

'*You silly old darling, don't trouble your head about things,*' replied Florence.

It was immediately assumed, by all who heard the nurse's report, how this latter conversation referred to James knowing he had been poisoned by his wife. But, could it have been about her affair with Alfred?

The next day, Saturday 11 May, Florence was banned from the sickroom. She collapsed and was put to bed. Later that evening, James died. Everybody in the household believed he had been poisoned by Florence and a witch hunt began to find evidence to substantiate their suspicions.

In the following hours, arsenic was found, supposedly hidden in a trunk containing the children's clothes: wrapped up in a handkerchief in her dressing gown pocket: more was found in a man's hat box. Nobody ever asked why did she hide this arsenic, which she had recently bought? If indeed she had hidden it. And, with all the arsenic and other poisons in the house, why was it necessary to buy some more? Just to murder her husband?

As there was already a plentiful supply of the poison used by James, and lying around just for the taking, why did she not use some of these if murdering James was her intention? The inference was the household was acting as judge, jury and executioner.

Arsenic was found in the meat juice James had been given and because there was more in the house, the doctor would not issue a death certificate.

The domestic staff did not like Florence. His brothers had mixed views. Matilda Briggs, through her previous relationship with James, was not Florence's friend, yet she almost came and went as she wanted to Battlecrease House. It would be fair to say Florence was a long way from home and a foreigner with few friends. And, whilst all this searching was taking place, she was semi-conscious and in no position to either witness the search of her belongings or answer any questions about what was found.

The police were informed, and a preliminary *autopsy* was conducted on James, in his bed. It only discovered how an unspecified irritant poison had caused *gastroenteritis*, from which he had died. He was buried on 16 May and exhumed on 18 May for another autopsy, but this time in secret. The suggestion already being any potential prosecution case was weak and the authorities were determined to prove Florence had murdered James.

This time traces of arsenic were found, but they were considered insufficient to have caused his death.

Nevertheless, on the strength of this latest evidence, Florence, was charged with her husband's murder.

In due course she appeared at the Liverpool Assizes.

The case for the Crown was her motive for poisoning James was in order to develop her affair with Alfred. Her defence, ably conducted by Charles Russell, a leading QC of the day, established how Florence was seeking a divorce from James, so there was no need to kill him. If so, where was her motive for killing him?

The means was cited as arsenic. But medical opinion admitted arsenic was used in many medicines of the day, both in those prescribed and those available over the counter. And there was insufficient arsenic found in his body to have killed him.

Matilda Briggs made an interesting witness.

She confirmed that a desk where arsenic had been found, was only ever used by James. The hat box, behind James's bed where more arsenic was found, only contained men's hats. Other places where arsenic was found, had not been hidden away. Dr Carter was adamant the cause of death was arsenic poisoning. Yet, he admitted never having treated anyone for such a complaint and had never attended an autopsy where arsenic was the cause of death.

Dr Stevenson, lecturer in toxicology at Guy's Hospital, London, confirmed the total amount of arsenic he found in James was 91/1000th of a grain – about 1/20th of the commonly accepted dose of two grains needed to cause death.

Edward Davies was the chemical analyst who managed to find just 1/50th of a grain of arsenic in James's body, and which with the other samples found, would only have equated to 1/8th of a grain. This amounted to about half of the smallest quantity he had previously found in a body.

It was never proved what killed James. This being the case, the Crown failed to prove means.

Edwin had instructed the nurses that they alone were to treat James and feed him. So, how had the poison, assuming it was poison, been administered? This also could not be answered, and the Crown failed to prove opportunity.

The chemist, who had sold the flypapers, agreed arsenic was used in cosmetics.

When cross-examined, Alice Yapp agreed Florence had acted quite openly when she transferred the medicine bottle's contents. She was far more reticent when it came to the affair of the letter. Many of her answers were vague or not answered at all. Strangely the judge came to her rescue, which led to later claims about his being biased against Florence. She was unable to explain why the letter, supposedly fallen in the wet, had not suffered from the ink running. Although being pressed on the point, she denied being a nosy parker who had opened the letter, just because of the identity of its recipient.

With the conclusion of the Crown case, it was time for the defence. Here Charles Russell had a problem.

Being 1889, defendants were still not permitted to give evidence on their own behalf on oath. Sometimes they were permitted to produce a written statement, but they could not be cross-examined or led through their evidence-in-chief. However, Mr Justice Stephen agreed Florence could make a verbal statement, in court, but without being allowed to read from any pre-prepared notes.

Florence stressed she had only added powders to medicines at her husband's requests, including the meat juice, but totally denied knowing what the powders were. She admitted using arsenic for cosmetic purposes, stressing the importance of keeping air from it, hence her handkerchief being used.

Infuriatingly, she told the court about being forgiven by James for the great wrong she had done him. Did she mean her infidelity or the poisoning? Because she could not be questioned, that will always remain a mystery. But, as she was pleading not guilty, it would be more likely to refer to the infidelity.

Other defence witnesses were called, mainly emphasizing the medical side of the case, before it was time for the summing up. To start with, Mr Justice Stephen seemed to be steering the jury towards an acquittal, because of the lack of evidence for the cause of death. Then he spent much time attacking her morals, especially referring to her affair with Alfred.

It took the jury just over half-an-hour to find her guilty and the death sentence inevitably followed.

The result created an absolute uproar.

Even allowing for forensic science available in 1889, the Crown had failed to prove, conclusively, that James had been poisoned. Several potential witnesses for the prosecution had not been called. Likewise, others had been missed by the defence. Generally speaking, there was great upset throughout the land following the result of the trial. Many considered the judge at fault for a biased summing up. He retired on grounds of ill-health soon after and finally died in 1894, whilst an inmate of a lunatic asylum.

There was a furious uproar from the medical fraternity.

Not only had the Crown failed to prove arsenic had caused James's death, they had been unable to show what had, let alone who had done it and how. Suicide or accident could not be ruled out. Whilst not proving the actual poison might have been acceptable in 1781 (Rex vs John Donellan) it was not in 1889.

Three days before her execution, Florence was awakened in the early hours of the morning, to be told her sentence had been commuted to life imprisonment. The general legal opinion was she was now in prison, for an offence for which she had never been tried, let alone found guilty.

The attempted murder of James, luckily for her no longer a capital crime.

Unfortunately for Florence, there was no mechanism in England for a retrial to be ordered and she remained in prison until her release in 1904. Queen Victoria would not countenance a pardon.

Her mother, now the Baroness von Roques never ceased fighting for her release. She had many supporters. The Baroness travelled twice a month from France to see her daughter. Sadly, whilst in prison, Florence's son, forbade his sister, Gladys, to have any more communication with their mother. Alfred Brierley left the country, and she never saw him again. Florence died in 1941, whilst living in Connecticut.

Her case is still a topic for discussion.

Did she or did she not poison her husband will always remain a mystery. The cause of his death has never been established, and clearly it was not the amount of arsenic he had in his body. So, perhaps, just perhaps, it could have been natural causes. Or, if it was murder, then who caused it and what was used? Alternatively, it could have been a genuine accident, brought about by his self-dosing of poison?

Whilst Florence must remain a suspect, what remains unanswered are the actions of the servants, the brothers and Matilda Briggs.

The servants did not like Florence, and neither did Matilda Briggs, but would that have been enough to make them poison James and put the blame on her? Possibly, but unlikely. They would be more likely to blame Florence for his death, because of their animosity and as a possible, malicious way of getting rid of her. If so, then their plan was successful, but it came at a price.

There are suggestions the brothers did not get on with James. Perhaps they hoped to gain from his death, even more so if the blame could be put onto Florence. In fact, the children were the main benefactors from his death. With the exception of some insurance policies, and income from property, albeit not very much, they inherited everything. Only the policies and house income were to go to Florence, who could never receive them. There was certainly some panic in the house when James died as to where his money and other assets were.

Author's comments

Was Florence as wicked as she is portrayed?

The Crown were unable to prove motive, means and opportunity. By today's standards, the evidence was very sparse and barely circumstantial. It seemed the authorities had decided she was guilty and needed to make the jury think so. There was ill-feeling and resentment towards her. The Crown undoubtedly relied on this ill-feeling to support its case. Despite tearing the main forensic witness to shreds, the defence could have done better, and certainly called more witnesses.

Perhaps Charles Russell thought an acquittal would be automatic and there was no need for anything else to be done. Who knows?

Was Florence wilful? I think the answer is yes. She was strong minded and was not going to let anybody take her for granted. Perhaps she was driven to act this way by living in Liverpool, with hostile staff, family and her husband's former fiancée?

She was certainly unconventional and quite prepared to flaunt her affair with Alfred Brierley in front of James. But then it can be argued so was James with his string of women. Yet, this was late Victorian England and her liberal attitude, especially from a female, would not have endeared her to many people.

Whatever the truth of James Maybrick's death, I am inclined to think she genuinely was not guilty and thus not wicked. The quantity of arsenic was so small, and he could easily have ingested it from his medicines, and it stayed in the human body for a matter of days or even longer. It is usually detected in urine, but none was found in James's samples. Had she been acquitted, I do not doubt she would have still been classed as wicked for her relationship with Alfred Brierly.

Recently, James Maybrick has come to the fore, as a main suspect for being Jack the Ripper. Allegedly, his diary, proving this to be true, was found at Battlecrease House, adding yet another dimension to the long running James and Florence Maybrick Saga.

The conspiracy theory is Jack the Ripper was causing all manner of problems in London and with there being no evidence to arrest James, other than being in London at the times of the murders, more drastic measures were needed.

Consequently, James Maybrick was judiciously murdered, and Florence set up to take the blame. Hence the unfairness of her trial! I do not believe such a tale.

I believe Florence Maybrick did not receive a fair trial. A recent television programme of legal experts agreed the verdict was unsafe. Her scandalous reputation had to be a disadvantage and the judge was biased against Florence. The scant evidence against her was barely circumstantial and I believe if this case appeared today, it would be rejected at the committal stage. It can be argued her subsequent imprisonment, without trial, contravened Magna Carta.

Florence's case, however, changed English Law, albeit too late to help her.

1898 saw the first time a defendant gave evidence on their own behalf, on oath, at a trial. 1907 saw the birth of the Appeal Court, whereby a convicted person was given the right to have their case reviewed.

Perhaps Queen Victoria should have the last words.

She considered it was acceptable for men to have mistresses but not for women to act in the same way.

28

Lady Harriett Sarah Mordaunt
née Moncreiffe (1848-1906)

In 1868, Sir Charles Mordaunt, from Walton Hall, near Stratford-upon-Avon, Warwickshire, was salmon fishing in Norway, but so far it had not been a particularly enjoyable experience.

In common with many of his peers, he preferred fishing there in preference to Scotland for various reasons, cost being one of them. The crossing had been rough, but worse was to come when he checked his fishing tackle for the first time. He had been sent the wrong line by his supplier. Then the weather was unbearably hot and much more to the point, he missed his young wife, Harriett. Consequently, he cut short his holiday and returned home two weeks earlier than originally arranged.

His original intention was to arrive on the Thursday, but he changed his mind and decided to come earlier and his give her a surprise. She had received a telegram about his Thursday homecoming and planned accordingly.

But when Charles arrived unexpectedly during the afternoon of Wednesday 15 July 1868, he certainly surprised Harriett, but not as either had anticipated. The events of that afternoon resulted in what is known as *The Warwickshire Scandal*.

Charles Mordaunt married Harriett Sarah Moncrieffe in December 1866 at Perth, Scotland, and brought her back to Walton Hall. Both remained part of the *Marlborough House Set* and socialized with people such as Edward, Prince of Wales and his wife.

It seemed initially, they were a happy couple, but later revelations told how Harriett entertained male guests, sometimes alone, whilst her husband was away. She had known Edward for some time and on occasions went to functions he had arranged in Scotland and London.

For instance, she would go to London with Charles, who was the Member of Parliament for South Warwickshire. At least once a week, when he was detained in the House of Commons, she entertained Edward alone in her hotel. Harriett also regularly wrote to him and he replied.

Charles was undoubtedly the main contender for her hand, but when marriage was first suggested, she hesitated. When he asked why, Harriet explained how the thoughts of living in the country, far away from London and other more entertaining places, was the problem. Desperate not to lose her, he agreed she could invite her friends to Walton Hall.

It is doubtful if Charles realized just then, how he had played into her hands. For a while he chose to ignore the warnings and advice he was being given about the Prince and Harriett being too close to each other. But after a while, relations between him and Edward started to cool. Furthermore, he began restricting some of the time Harriett spent away from home.

There can be little doubt he loved her.

Whilst Charles was away fishing in Norway, and unbeknown to him, she had been entertaining at Walton Hall. Amongst her visitors were Edward and Lord Lowry Cole, later 4th Earl of Enniskillen. Following the non-delivery of the telegram from Charles advising her of his change of plans, Harriett had planned to carry on entertaining them for another fourteen days before he returned. When the next telegram arrived, announcing his change of plans, she only had two days before his return. Most of her guests left quickly, believing he would not want to find a house full on his return.

Still believing she had an extra day, one of her guests stayed on, blissfully unaware Charles was already on his way home.

Charles arrived on that fateful afternoon and made his way to the courtyard, where he was totally unprepared for what he found.

He quickly recognized the small carriage Harriett was driving and pulled by two white ponies which had been a gift from the Prince. Harriett was showing off her driving skills and looking fondly at the shadowy figure of a man standing in front of the Hall. A man who was obviously impressed by Harriett and what he was seeing. Charles had no problem in recognizing him.

It was Albert Edward, Prince of Wales and future King Edward VII.

As can be imagined, Charles was furious and grew even more so when he recalled the warnings, which had been given earlier about Edward's association with Harriett.

Words were said and the Prince stormed off, allegedly on foot into the nearby village of Walton, where he found a carrier who would take him to Moreton-in-Marsh railway station.

Meanwhile, Charles had the two white ponies shot in front of Harriett and ordered the carriage to be burnt, although it is believed it was spirited away and sold to a Stratford plumber.

There have been suggestions made about the two ponies not being shot, but quietly sold. The author was giving this presentation once when a member of the audience spoke. She had been at Walton Hall visiting a relative on the staff, when some excavation work was being carried out. In the process, the skeletons of two small ponies, were found. Each of them had been shot in the head.

Rightly or wrongly everyone assumed they were Harriett's two ponies

During the next few days, Charles and Harriett had some sort of truce before going to Scotland. Nevertheless, it was abundantly clear he could never trust her to be left alone again for any lengthy periods. Likewise, her visits to London would be limited. Charles was content he would have very little, if any, further communications with the Prince. He would certainly not descend again, unannounced and uninvited to Walton Hall whilst Charles was away. It was also clear there would be a General Election in the Autumn, which gave him the perfect excuse to leave Parliament.

Despite these problems, the future looked good, but it could not last.

Less than nine months after her husband's surprise return, Harriett gave birth to a daughter and tried to explain Violet as being premature. It was a good idea, but the child was too far developed for a premature birth and was clearly conceived whilst Charles was in Norway.

Faced with no other option. Harriett confessed to Charles he was not Violet's father. Her words said how she had been *'very wicked and done wrong.'* As if that was not bad enough, worse followed and Charles cannot have anticipated the full extent of her answer to his next and obvious question. *'Who is Violet's father?'*

Whilst he expected such a dubious honour would go to the Prince, Charles never anticipated the list of names which followed of men who *might* be her father. These included the Prince, Lord Cole, Sir Frederick Johnstone and others, to name but a few.

In other words, Harriett admitted she did not know who was Violet's father.

Regardless of the ensuing scandal, Charles had no alternative but to sue for divorce. Here the story took on another twist and there is still some doubt as to Harriett's ensuing claims to insanity.

When Harriett became pregnant, she was still only twenty years old and her husband twelve years older. She was clearly very upset by Violet's arrival especially when there was no chance of a premature birth explanation being accepted. Harriet was now in serious trouble and obviously thought confessing to Charles, before he learnt the truth, was the best option. Perhaps, just perhaps she might have survived had she only named the Prince as the father, so the matter could have been quietly hushed up. Her whole behavior during this period and afterwards is best described as erratic.

It is doubtful if such a scheme would have worked. Queen Victoria was not impressed by her son's philandering ways and it is very doubtful if she would have helped either him or Harriett.

Her claiming to have had sexual relations with other men, effectively put a stop to just blaming Edward. It also started people wondering about the mental state of her mind. When Charles later petitioned for divorce, her mental state played a big part.

Her family claimed she was mentally unbalanced in the hope the matter could be shut up, and Harriett allowed to quietly return to Scotland. Charles, feeling very betrayed, totally disagreed and counter claimed whilst his wife was obviously distressed, she was faking insanity. He would have known insanity was not grounds for a divorce.

Some of her activities to make people believe she was insane included calling for a servant who was not there; engage in periods of not speaking to anyone: wearing the wrong clothes such as outdoor ones inside the Hall. On the other hand, she wrote a letter to Charles just a few days before the hearing, which gave no hint of lunacy.

Then the Prince interfered.

Deeply concerned about the strong possibility of a scandal, he sent two doctors, including William Gull, to see her. They arrived unannounced and formed the opinion she was of an unsound mind.

Unwillingly, the Prince was subpoenaed and very reluctantly testified. His evidence was restricted to verifying his handwriting on certain letters. He steadfastly denied any improper behaviour with Harriett and denied being Violet's father.

Having weighed up all the evidence, the judge finally agreed, and Harriett was considered unfit to plead. Possibly this might have been what Harriett planned if she had been faking insanity. If it was, then the outcome would not have been what she had envisaged.

She was released into her husband's care and moved away from Walton Hall into a succession of houses and private asylums. Whilst divorce, at least for the moment was out of the question, so was being released into her family's care.

If the Prince, other members of the *Marlborough House Set* and Harriett's family thought this was the end of the affair, they were to be sadly mistaken.

Charles had not finished yet.

In May 1874, he appealed to the House of Lords on the vexed question: was lunacy a bar to divorce? A majority decision of 3:2 agreed it was not. As soon as he heard the news, Charles instructed his lawyers to commence divorce proceedings against Harriett on the grounds of adultery. Despite his wishes, they advised it would not be a good idea to cite the Prince and others. They were not interested in how much he disagreed, and Charles had to settle for Lord Cole.

The lawyers admitted they wanted to limit the media interest in the case and insisted no damages would be claimed. In fact, their decisions did very little to reduce the notoriety which the case had already gathered.

Shortly before the trial started, Lord Cole admitted he was Violet's father, and a divorce followed. No doubt Charles was happy with the result, but not with how it had come about. With no witnesses needing to be called, the Prince escaped with his reputation intact, which defeated Charles's plans to expose him.

We shall never know if Cole really was Violet's father. Had he taken the blame to let the Prince avoid much notoriety? Quite possibly the answer was yes.

Harriett spent the remainder of her life in one form of asylum or another. Regardless of all she had done, Charles still had to pay for her maintenance. In early 1877, Harriett was just known as Miss Moncreiffe and it must have been a happy release when she died in 1906.

Charles ignored Violet and she was brought up by Harriett's family. Money for her maintenance came from the settlement he had made on Harriett. Violet married the 5th Marquess of Bath, but neither of her parents attended the wedding.

It is possible they were not invited.

Charles later married Mary Louisa, fondly known as Maimée because she was liked by all, second daughter of the Hon. Henry Pitt Cholmondeley, in 1878. Unlike, her predecessor, she was not interested in a hectic social life and happily adapted to living at Walton Hall with their son and five daughters. The arrival of his children put paid to the long-standing rumours about him being sterile.

Sadly, Charles died following complications from a fall in 1897. He was deeply mourned by Maimée, his family, all his tenants and many other people.

Author's comments

Was Harriett a wicked woman?

In her own words, yes, she was. She had no regard for her marriage vows, but in Victorian times, having affairs was the order of the day in some sections of society. But having children by a lover who was not your husband? Not so clear cut.

When I first came across her case, several years ago, I felt she was naïve and had been seduced by the Prince and to be pitied more than blamed. But as I researched more deeply, my opinion has changed. Despite her youth, I am quite convinced Harriett knew what she was doing, and the question is, was she a **nymphomaniac**? Or was Charles not so good in bed?

I think she liked the intrigue and having sex with influential people whilst two-timing her husband. Certainly, most of her forays were planned, either at home or elsewhere, such the Prince's visit whilst Charles was in Norway.

What, if anything, did she know about birth control? I suggest not a lot or more probably nothing. Becoming pregnant must have been a shock. Did she really believe Charles could be the father? I suspect it was wishful thinking. She hung on to this belief and a premature birth, until told in no certain terms the child was too far advanced for such an excuse to work.

Clearly this is when she began to panic and possibly thought about trying to save her marriage. Had she just stuck to one man being the father, it might have convinced Charles. But, by her own admission, she did not know who the father was!

Harriett was certainly wilful and unconventional: someone who went against many of the conventions imposed when indulging in extra-marital affairs.

Finally, there is the question of her insanity as it was called then. Was it genuine or feigned?

There are suggestions it was feigned to help her case, when it came to the divorce court as it surely would. Charles believed her family were involved and encouraged her to act the part. The insanity claim was helped tremendously by the Prince's own doctors agreeing she was of unsound mind. It also helped to get him off the hook.

If it had been an act, then it backfired on her horrendously.

It would not be the first time when someone has played the mental health card only to have the pretended problems become real.

Whatever the facts of the case, I believe there is little doubt she was mentally ill at the time of her death. This is probably not surprising when we think what her life must have been like living under restraint in various lunatic asylums, to use the expressions of the day.

Harriett was a good time girl who enjoyed her life to the full without any forward thinking or consideration for other people. She had married into an enviable way of life with property, lands and servants, then lost it at an incredibly young age through her own stupidity. And which resulted in her being treated as insane for nearly sixty years.

I find Harriett Mordaunt more selfish, wilful and unconventional rather than wicked. Nevertheless, I have very little sympathy for her.

29

Alma Victoria Rattenbury *née* Clarke; *aka* Dolling, *aka* Pakenham (1892-1935) and George Percy Stoner (1917-2000)

Alma's origins remain confused.

It is thought she was born in 1892, but her birth was not registered until 1897. She later changed her middle name from Belle to Victoria and was always reticent about her true age.

What was never in doubt, was her sensuality, and exceptional beauty. Added to these attractions was a talent for playing and composing music. Having lost her first husband during the First World War, she joined an ambulance unit, and saw service at the Front. During this period, she was wounded twice and awarded the Croix de Guerre with Star and Palm, by the French Government.

At the end of the war, she met and fell in love with Captain Compton Pakenham. Unfortunately, he was already married. Not that it mattered too much as a divorce followed with Alma being named in the proceedings. Once he was free, they married in 1921, but it was over two years later, and their divorce followed. With her mother's help, Alma and her young son Christopher moved to Canada.

Alma was at a function there in 1923, when she first met Francis Rattenbury. It was a meeting which was to fatally change both their lives.

Francis Mawson Rattenbury was born in Leeds in 1867. In his youth he had driven cattle to Dawson City, in the Klondike, at the time of the 1898 Gold Rush and no doubt made a considerable amount of money in the process.

No one ever understood why they fell for each other.

He was a famous architect, whilst she was about half his age with a scandalous reputation. She was a very attractive woman who showed an interest in him. Had he been flattered by her attention? Or had she seen him as a good financial bet? Who knows? Whatever the reason, they were soon involved in a torrid love affair.

From being just an affair, their relationship turned more serious and marriage was discussed.

But there was a big problem. Francis was already married to Florence Nunn, who did not want a divorce.

Not that Alma was at all worried. To make matters worse, when he moved out of their marital home, in what can be called an act of petty spite, Francis had the heating and lights turned off. Finally, only too aware he was not going to give Alma up, Florence agreed to a divorce in 1925. Once it was all settled, Francis and Alma wasted no time in getting married.

Francis soon found the bullying tactics he had used against Florence, did not win him any friends. In fact, the opposite happened.

Alma's reputation was now in ruins and it has been suggested she had become a drug addict, with the reputation of being a man eater. Francis was largely ignored by his former friends and missing out on business opportunities, because of his divorce and subsequent marriage to Alma. Although Francis had fathered their son John, in 1928, he discovered being married to her was not all he had expected. Having ruined his previous good name to possess her, he must have started having second thoughts.

Ultimately, they moved to England, after making several expensive detours. In early 1930, Alma, Francis and John, came to live at the Villa Madeira, 5 Manor Road, Bournemouth.

It was a move which had fatal consequences.

Alma was now frustrated in more ways than one.

Since John's birth, she had not enjoyed any marital relations with Francis.

She lacked companionship because he was ageing, becoming deaf and turning to alcohol. Despite the cost, as Francis was always complaining about his wife's extravagant ways, she employed Irene Riggs as a servant, who soon became her confidante.

It is fair to say Irene was concerned about Alma's way of life.

Alma's music career enjoyed a partial revival, but it never progressed as well as she would have liked. Whilst it was easy to criticize Francis for his irritating ways, she also had her own strange habits. These included not getting dressed in the morning and spending the day in her pyjamas. Another habit involved her drinking more and more heavily as the hours progressed.

It is well recorded how highly sexed Alma was, although there is no evidence of her having any extra marital affairs since her marriage. There may have been some casual flings (or one-night stands), and several male members of staff left, apparently after she had tried to seduce them. She also had suffered from **pulmonary tuberculosis,** which has been blamed for heightening her sexual appetite. As for Francis, he now drank most of a bottle of whisky each night.

When the latest male servant left in September 1934, Alma and Francis decided they must advertise for another, only this time they stipulated he had to be aged between fourteen and eighteen, and preferably with boy scout experience. George Percy Stoner (17), who lacked both qualifications, but being able to drive, was given the post.

If Irene had hoped Stoner was too young for her mistress, she was soon disillusioned.

Not long after Stoner started, Alma took him to Oxford, where they stayed together at the Randolph Hotel. She had supposedly been going to visit her relatives in Sunderland and it could be argued Oxford was on the way.

At some stage during this trip, Alma seduced him. Thereafter she had a full-time lover, and their affair developed rapidly. Before too long, Alma had arranged for him to sleep in the house: most nights in her bed. Neither of them seemed worried about their affair becoming common knowledge.

Irene was soon aware of what was happening and tried to convince Alma of its folly and how she was playing with fire. Had Alma listened to her advice, matters would have turned out much differently. Stoner was believed to be taking *cocaine*, and the general inference was Alma gave it to him. To be fair, this has always been something of a grey area, and cannot be taken as the absolute truth.

As the new year dawned, matters started drawing to their dramatic and tragic close.

On 15 March 1935, Alma persuaded Francis to give her £250 (approximately £12,660 today). She stressed it was to pay for an operation on her glands. Somewhat reluctantly he parted with the money. Undoubtedly, he would not have done so, had he known the real reason for her wanting it.

She used part of it to pay off her overdraft and settling some of her other debts. Once that was done, she and Stoner went to London where she spent the balance on him and herself. The journey had its own problems. When having only travelled as far as Southampton, the car broke down and they had to finish their journey by train.

Officially they stayed at their hotel as brother and sister, but she spent a lot of money on buying him clothes, doing the sights and dining well. For someone of Stoner's lowly background and upbringing, such a way of life, albeit only for a few days, must have been an unbelievable experience. It gave him a taste of the good life, which he did not want to end and was not one he would give up easily. They returned on Friday 22 March and all was well for a few hours, but not for long.

Everything changed over the weekend.

On the Sunday, Francis suggested they should go to Bridport, to see one of his friends and then stay the night. Hearing of these arrangements, Stoner became very jealous. He was most unhappy at the prospects of his mistress sharing a bed with her husband.

It was, by any stretch of the imagination, a strange way of life for all three of them. They were a *ménage-à-trois*, although only she and Stoner had sex. Francis was now impotent and generally too inebriated at night to contemplate having sex with anyone, let alone his wife. The servants knew what was happening and so must Francis. Assuming that was so, then he must have condoned the arrangement. Nevertheless, what was practiced in the Villa Madeira where they lived, could not be countenanced in a friend's house.

Stoner did not see it that way and lost his temper. He maintained if they went, then he would refuse to take them. At which point he stormed out of the house, in a very agitated state of mind.

What happened next has never been fully explained and still remains a mystery.

Alma left Francis at about 9.0pm and retired upstairs to bed as Francis always slept downstairs. She stated when Stoner joined her later in the bedroom, he seemed to be very agitated and kept on saying they would not be going to Bridport. At about 10.30pm, he became very quiet. Suspecting he had done something silly Alma went downstairs which was where she found Francis.

He was slumped in a chair, but with severe wounds to his head. In due course Doctor O'Donnell arrived and had Francis removed to hospital. Then he informed the police.

During the early hours of Monday morning, PC Arthur Ernest Bagwell was the first of several police officers from Bournemouth police station, then policed by Hampshire, to arrive at a very bizarre scene.

They all agreed Alma appeared to be drunk. Every light was on in the house and the gramophone was playing loudly. She also tried to kiss most of them when they arrived. In total she made four statements that night. In one she admitted having hit Francis. She was arrested later that day. Soon afterwards Francis died and Alma was charged with his murder by Detective Inspector William Carter.

Meanwhile Stoner had disappeared.

Stoner returned to the Villa Madeira four days later and spoke to Irene Riggs. He explained it was his intention to sleep that night in the house and then give himself up the next morning. Bizarrely he asked her to wake him in good time. Irene agreed, but telephoned the police as soon as it was safe to so. They came and arrested him later that evening and he was duly charged with murdering Francis.

During their subsequent trial at the Old Bailey, Alma denied making a statement about having hit Francis. Perhaps she did not actually deny hitting him but maintained she could not remember doing so. Being drunk and under sedation from Dr O'Donnell at the time, she might have been telling the truth. Stoner declined to testify. Alma was referred to as a *nymphomaniac*, which was possibly true.

She was defended by Terence James O'Connor, who was ably assisted by Ewen Edward Samuel Montagu, second son of Lord Swayling. He would ultimately serve in Naval Intelligence during the Second World War and be responsible for *The Man Who Never Was* plan, codenamed *Operation Mincemeat*, which fooled the Germans over the invasion of Sicily in 1943.

Despite trying to take the blame to protect her lover, the jury found Alma not guilty, but Stoner was not so lucky. It was proved he had borrowed a mallet from his grandparents and used it to kill Francis. He was found guilty and sentenced to death.

At the time of her trial, Alma was regarded with total revulsion by everybody. Probably she was ill, and a drug addict and tried to take the blame on herself right away, although she denied making the statement confessing to hitting him. Was this possibly in a misguided attempt to protect Stoner? By the time Alma left the Old Bailey, she was clearly very mentally unbalanced. Three days later, determined to be re-united with her lover in death, she took her own life in Hampshire.

Even in death Alma retained her flamboyancy as she stabbed herself, which is not the easiest or most painless of self-inflicted deaths.

Stoner's case went to appeal, but the conviction was upheld. Yet, because of his age, he was reprieved from being hanged, and sentenced to penal servitude, from which he was ultimately released. By then, Alma had long since killed herself.

Stoner only served seven years in prison before he was released and fought in the Second World War. He died in 2000 aged eighty-three and always refused to discuss the case.

Author's comments

Was Alma Rattenbury wicked?

It is easy to blame her confused and possibly drugged mental state for all what happened, but was she in such a state before the fatal affair with George Stoner? I would suggest Alma knew exactly what she was doing. She needed sex, which was something Francis could no longer give her, but Stoner could. And it seems Francis was happy with the arrangement. But did this *ménage-à-trois* make her wicked?

Undoubtedly Florence Rattenbury and Compton Pakenham's wife would have thought she was wicked for destroying their marriages.

Alma was wilful and unconventional.

Throughout her life, she was only interested in herself. Husbands two and three along the way were for her to use and dispose of when ready. Although, if we accept her innocence, she never intended Francis being murdered. Had a stranger been responsible then it would have been a tremendous stroke of luck.

The big question remains: did she have any involvement in her husband's murder? I suspect not. Her involvement came after it had happened.

Was she really so drunk? Why was the gramophone playing so loudly? Was she trying to deflect any blame away from Stoner and put it on herself? If so, was she trying to establish a mental problem that may or may not have existed?

The motive for her to murder Francis would be to get him permanently out of the way so she could marry Stoner. I suggest this is very tenuous as the *ménage-à-trois* was working without any real problems until Stoner's jealousy caused by the proposed trip to Bridport.

The means obviously was to club him to death with the mallet. Very few women murderers use force, preferring more subtle means such as poison. There was no evidence to prove she had acquired the mallet and subsequently used it.

If she needed an opportunity to murder him, it could have happened at any time, not just on that night.

I believe his murder was not her idea, but Stoner is a different story.

His motive being jealousy. He acquired the means by borrowing the mallet which he used to devastating effect. His opportunity came after Alma had gone to bed leaving Francis alone downstairs and well under the influence of drink as usual.

Going to get the mallet made this a pre-meditated murder.

Had Alma not been so impetuous and taken her own life, she could have waited for her lover to be released, and then be free to marry him. But, would she really have wanted that? He was a mere chauffeur, from a working-class background, and she was old enough to be his mother? I suspect not because he did not have any money, but neither did she. Her money, such as it was, came from Francis. With the style of life she enjoyed, could this ever have worked? In many ways it would have been a complete reversal of her marriage to Francis.

And the mystery still remains today.

Who really murdered Francis? Whilst Alma had to be a suspect, it is unlikely, although not impossible she did so. The most likely suspect has to be Stoner. If so, did he do it of his own volition, or at Alma's instigation or even with her help? Whichever it was, Alma must take the blame for it happening. Had she not seduced Stoner this tragic murder would probably never had happened. I suggest she was wicked, wilful and unconventional.

We shall never know what really happened, that night in Bournemouth.

Much speculation remains, even today, about the effect Edith Thompson's execution in 1923, had on this case. Edith's guilty verdict had not been well received, and neither was her subsequent hanging. With Alma's trial, Edith's case was resurrected, complete with concerns about not repeating another unfair verdict. Possibly, just possibly, this might have had some influence on the jury's decision to acquit Alma.

30

Olivia *aka* Olive Serres *née* Wilmot *aka* Princess of Cumberland (1772-1834)

Always known as Olive, she was allegedly born at Warwick on 3 April 1772 in St John's House and baptized a few days later at St Nicholas Church. Her recorded father, Robert Wilmot, was a talented artist. Following allegations of embezzlement whilst he was the Warwickshire County treasurer, the family was evicted from St John's House. Robert and his wife Anna went to London, leaving Olive behind in the care of her uncle, the Reverend Dr James Wilmot. He was rector of the Warwickshire village of Barton-on-the-Heath, near Stratford-upon-Avon and who played a part in what later happened to Olive.

In 1776, two volumes of anonymous letters were published under the title of *The Letters of Junius,* which were very critical of George III's Government. Following his death in 1807, Olive suggested her uncle might have been the author. The true identity of this writer remains unknown.

Olive's stay with him was not without incident.

One evening when her uncle was away, the rectory was burgled. Olive maintained she had been nailed up in her bedroom whilst the villains tied up the servants, ransacked the building, then helped themselves to food and drink. Finally, the seventeen-year-old Olive explained how she had escaped by climbing out of a window and raising the alarm. Two of the gang were arrested and thanks to her testimony were hanged. Despite being regarded as the hero of the day, there were lingering doubts. Neighbours had heard her firing a single shot for no apparent reason, just before the burglary took place. As Olive knew the hanged men, had the shot been a signal to them?

This was an early instance of people considering her to be a liar, and was a reputation destined to follow her until she died. Having worn out her welcome in Warwickshire, Olive moved to London soon afterwards.

Here she continued her notoriety.

Already possessing some talent, she became a pupil of artist John Thomas Serres. They married later in what was to be a disastrous marriage. Olive was an attractive woman and her subsequent actions ensured she had a string of lovers and illegitimate children. In next to no time, she had acquired the nickname of 'The Warwick(shire) Pop-Lolly'. This was an obvious reference to a sweet meat but with sexual overtones.

As expected in eighteenth century London, she moved around in society circles and became friends with George Greville, the impoverished 2nd Earl of Warwick following the title's recreation in 1759. When his debts became too heavy, he was evicted from Warwick Castle and trustees put in charge. During this time, Olive supported him financially, but it all went wrong when he failed to meet any of his financial obligations.

Trying to make amends, he gave her a bundle of documents with strict instructions how they were not to be read until George III had died.

As early as 1817, Olive had heard rumours about her supposed real ancestry. It was suggested Robert and Anna Wilmot were not her real parents. Olive now believed she was of royal blood and was in fact the daughter of the Duke of Cumberland. And if true, she was entitled to be called the Princess of Cumberland. Nevertheless, her approaches to the Royal Family were well and truly rebuffed. Undeterred, Olive now styled herself princess.

Using this title on one occasion stopped her immediate imprisonment for debt, not that she was a stranger to such an impecunious state.

When George III died in 1820, Olive opened the documents George Greville had given her.

These were almost unbelievable.

In brief, they related to a secret marriage between Dr James Wilmot and

Princess Poniatowski, sister of King Stanislaus I of Poland. There was a daughter from the union also called Olive. At face value, this made Olive Serres James's granddaughter and not his niece. In due course, this Olive secretly married Prince Henry Frederick, Duke of Cumberland and Strathearn. The ceremony was conducted in London by a certain Reverend Dr James Wilmot.

This was later disproved by the Palace, but nevertheless the story does not end there.

Henry Frederick was the youngest of George III's siblings and often referred to as *'the royal idiot'*. He was renowned for his numerous affairs and the Royal Marriages Act 1772 was almost certainly brought in because of him. In 1771 he had married Anne Horton a commoner, which caused all manner of friction between them and the Royal Family. When she gave birth to a baby girl, it was suggested her child was raised by Robert and Anna as their own daughter, at Warwick, and baptized as Olive Wilmot. If true, then Olive's earlier claim to be called princess now had more than a ring of truth about it. Olive also believed she stood in line to the throne.

But she had completely overlooked the provisions of The Royal Marriages Act 1772, which ensured only genuine and legitimate descendants of Sophie of Hanover could ascend to the Throne of England.

Was it co-incidence this legislation it was enacted in 1772? The same year the daughter of Henry Frederick Cumberland and Anne Horton, also known as Olive Serres was born?

Olive's claim all depended on how legitimate the marriage of her so-called parents had been. According to the letters supplied by the Earl of Warwick, the marriage had been legal and therefore she could be called princess. She further claimed she had been created Princess Cumberland by George III in 1773.

Totally convinced of her claim, Olive openly called herself Princess Cumberland and drove around in a carriage bearing the Royal Coat of Arms. The Royal Family were not impressed by her claims and kept their distance. Some doubt remained about whether George III had actually created her a princess, but he was dead and could not be questioned.

Olive produced various documents, which the Palace claimed were forgeries. Several of which have conveniently disappeared over the years. Was this an official cover up?

Undeterred, Olive pursued the matter through the courts. She had various allies, one of whom was the Duke of Kent who wished to marry her. The problem was she already had a husband.

A more influential friend was Joseph Wilfred Parkins, Sheriff of the City of London, and whose mistress she was. Whilst he could have been a useful ally, she took too much for granted and turned him into a formidable enemy. Always short of money she regularly borrowed from him. In his turn, he was happy to lend it to her. This feeling rapidly changed once he realized it would never be repaid and arguments followed. When she jilted him in favour of a younger man, it was a very bad mistake. Whilst he might have forgiven her the money, being jilted was an insult too far.

He sought revenge.

His first move was to write to Olive's husband complaining about his *'wicked and wasteful wife.'* Much to his surprise John Serres replied and agreed it was high time to put a stop to such *'fraudulent humbug.'* Serres also knew the Palace had launched an enquiry into the affair, and he was more than happy to assist them in any way he could.

One particularly damning piece of evidence came from the Pontiatowski family. They were adamant none of King Stanislaus's sisters had ever been to England. Other evidence confirmed Dr Wilmot had been at Oxford at the time of the so-called marriage of the Duke of Cumberland and his so-called daughter. If true, he could not have performed the ceremony

The commissioners finally agreed the documents were all forgeries and as far as they were concerned, her claim held no validity. She had not helped her cause by making scandalous attacks on the Royal Family, the same people she wanted to join. Her allegations included George IV stabbing a groom to death and the Duke of Kent committing adultery with his own sister. She accused more members of other sinful activities.

Olive never accepted the ruling and spent the rest of her days contesting it in between going to prison for debt. Following her death in 1834, Olive's daughter, styled herself Princess Lavinia and continued the fight.

She too failed.

Author's comments

Was Olive wicked?

It is not easy to describe her. Reports today differ about her various activities and probably are a mixture of fact, legend and conjecture.

If the suggestion she put the gang up to burgling the rectory and then testified against them is true, then her behavior is questionable. If such evidence led to their execution as her testimony did, then I think wicked does apply to her.

However, her activities in London were more varied and complicated. She was a romancer and quite unscrupulous. Her marriage vows to John Serres meant nothing to her and she used people to her own advantage. Undoubtedly, Olive had considerable sexual attraction to men which she used for own advancement. Money was always a pressing need and she used her considerable charms to wheedle it away from people.

We shall never know the truth of her birth. Was she really the daughter of Robert and Anna Wilmot? Or Henry Frederick Cumberland and Anne Horton? How does Dr James Wilmot fit into the picture?

It can certainly be argued Olive was bad in moral conduct with all her lovers and illegitimate children. Morally depraved could also fit in here.

Was Olive wilful?

I believe there can be no doubt she did exactly what she wanted to do regardless of who was hurt. Ironically, it was this treatment of John Serres and J.W. Parkins which led to her ultimate downfall. This is all evidence of her doing exactly what she wanted to do, rightly or wrongly. A mystery is why she put it about how Dr James Wilmot was the author of the *Letters of Junius* when there was nothing to support such a claim. Or was she paving the way to try and make her uncle (or grandfather) seem more important than he was when it came to the secret marriages?

Who had first suggested the idea of the Duke of Cumberland being her rightful father? Why did George Greville give her the documents? Did he believe them and was he perhaps trying to repay her earlier kindnesses to him?

Olive was unconventional. Her actions were not what would have been expected or accepted in late Georgian society. Yes, many men had mistresses, but as a rule they tried to keep the details quiet with varying degrees of success.

One question remains.

Did Olive honestly believe she was Princess Cumberland? Or had she lived the role for so long she actually believed it? I almost get the impression the Palace was not too worried about her claims and only stepping in when Olive kept persisting how she was of royal blood. Yet why was she permitted to drive around in a carriage displaying the Royal Coat of Arms?

Whatever the truth, the Palace finally contested her claims more seriously after the intervention of John Serres and J. W. Parkins. Even so, she continued to dispute their opinion and her daughter continued the struggle after 1834.

Perhaps, just perhaps, there might have been some truth in her claims although the Royal Marriages Act effectively put an end to any possibility of her ever ascending to the throne. It was if it had been passed with Olive Serres in mind.

I believe Olive Serres was wicked, wilful and unconventional.

31
Madeleine Hamilton Smith
aka Wardle (1835-1928)

Madeleine was the eldest and spoilt daughter of wealthy Glasgow architect James Smith. Described as a '*bright and attractive girl*,' she should have had no problems in finding male company, with the aim of acquiring a suitable husband.

Instead, and initially unbeknown to her parents, she started an affair with Pierre Emile L'Angelier, who worked in Glasgow as a clerk to a local seedsman. Regardless of her family's wealth this affair broke the Glasgow society conventions of the time. And when it was discovered a sensational scandal ensued.

Pierre came from St Helier, Jersey, and was twelve years older than Madeleine. He was nowhere near her equal socially nor in education and intelligence, nevertheless he considered himself to be irresistible to all women. Whilst this may have been true, until Madeleine came into his life most of his sexual encounters, had not been with classy women.

His one and albeit very brief venture into high society happened in Paris, during the 1848 Revolution and it gave him a taste for such a life. But lacking money and social background, it was an uphill and almost impossible task, to continue with this idea.

He needed to find a woman with money.

Some people have described him as '*charming, but rather weak*,' which worked to his advantage. Many women, especially older ones, wanted to mother him. Observers of the case have often thought he was looking for just such a marriage. Despite all these disadvantages, he must have had some attraction as Madeleine became besotted by him in 1855. Or, did she encourage him just for the fun, thrill and adventure of it to prove her own independence?

Whatever her reasons, she was just the sort of woman he sought: one who would ultimately inherit a great deal of money which he would be able to control.

Their romance began in secret, as Madeleine was under no illusions about how her father would react and totally oppose the idea. Consequently, they wrote regularly to each other and when they met, it had to be at a friend's house. Nevertheless, it was only a matter of time before her father discovered what was happening. When that happened, as expected, her father forbade her to see Pierre again.

Not that she worried too much about his orders. She knew only too well he was a weak-willed man and no match for his eldest daughter. Whatever she may have promised her father, Madeleine continued seeing Pierre in secret.

Finally, they arranged to elope, but, at the last minute she changed her mind. In early 1857, she became engaged to William Minnoch, a rich Glasgow merchant, and a wedding was arranged for June the same year. It was at this point she realized her affair with Pierre had to cease.

She quickly discovered to her dismay, how such an ending would be far easier said than done. Pierre knew when he was on to a good thing and had no intention of letting her go.

Having taken up with a prospective husband, Madeleine wrote to Pierre, and asked him to return all the love letters she had sent him, adding how she did not love him anymore. Whilst a few of these letters still survive, some doubt has been cast over their authenticity. If they are to be believed, they describe, in very graphic detail, the physical side of their relationship and highlight just how she enjoyed having sex.

Unsurprisingly, he declined to do as she asked and threatened to send them to her father. There was no suggestion at this point of any demands for money, only an implied threat to ruin her life if she would not take him back again. Madeleine wrote several more times, beseeching him to return the letters, but never received any replies.

Dates now become important, some of which have come from Pierre's diaries. He always referred to her as Mimi and she called him Emile.

Some time between 11 and 13 February 1857, Madeleine sent a servant to buy her some **prussic acid,** maintaining she needed it to treat a skin complaint, which would have been a genuine reason for wanting it. However, the chemist refused to serve him.

16 February, Pierre was taken ill.

19 February, Pierre saw Madeleine for a few minutes. In the meantime, she had written to him yet again asking for the letters to be returned, which he did not answer. He was ill again during the night, when Madeleine had gone to the theatre with William Minnoch.

20 February Pierre recorded having spent '*two pleasant hours*' with her.

21 February Pierre recorded '*don't feel well,*' in his diary. Madeleine purchased some **arsenic,** mixed with soot claiming it was for domestic use in the garden and house. She asked for this to be charged to her father's account and duly signed for it.

22 February, they met and later he wrote '*taken very ill*'.

27 February, Madeleine wrote and told him she was going away for the week.

4 March, they met again, and she advised him to leave Glasgow and go to England.

5 March, they exchanged notes. Pierre now accused her of being engaged to someone else and insisted on a satisfactory answer. He threatened to end their affair.

6 March, in company with a friend, she purchased more arsenic, mixed with indigo, from a different chemist to use as a rat poison. Later the same day she left for Bridge of Allan.

13 March, Madeleine wrote to Pierre, describing him as '*my own beloved sweet pet.*'

17 March, she returned to Glasgow.

18 March, she purchased more arsenic, mixed with soot, to kill rats.

19 March, and unbeknown to Madeleine, Pierre went to Bridge of Allan.

20-21 March, Madeleine wrote, asking to see Pierre immediately, not knowing he was at Bridge of Allan. This letter was not answered. She wrote again and this second letter was forwarded to him at his holiday address.

22 March, Pierre returned to Glasgow, but left his lodgings at 9.0pm, without telling his landlady where he was going, but saying he expected to return late.

23 March, he returned in the early hours, but was clearly seriously ill, and died later that morning. Madeleine's father was informed soon afterwards, by some of Pierre's friends, and fingers of suspicion were already being pointed at her. However, she denied having seen him during the past three weeks.

24 March, the doctors initially agreed there was no need for an *autopsy*, clearly convinced Pierre had died of natural causes.

26 March, Pierre was buried, and Madeleine disappeared. Her whereabouts were discovered later by friends.

31 March, Pierre's body was exhumed, and an autopsy discovered a large quantity of arsenic in his stomach. Suspicion naturally fell on Madeleine and she was committed to prison the same day. Her trial began at the Edinburgh High Court on 30 June and lasted until 9 July.

She was tried on two charges of attempted murder and one of murder, before an all-male jury. Female jurors did not sit in Scottish courts until 1921. The evidence against her was only circumstantial, and the Crown could not prove any meeting between the two when Pierre was first taken ill.

With the second illness, there was no evidence to prove it had been caused by poison. True, she had purchased arsenic, but it could not be proved they had met that day.

A similar situation existed for the night of his death. Nobody could prove they had met, although Pierre had been seen near her house, they had not been seen together. Whilst in court, she was supported by the masses, who thought very little of Pierre and showed little or no sympathy towards him.

The jury returned after twenty-five minutes and unanimously acquitted her of the first charge of attempted murder. On the other two charges, they returned a verdict of not proven; which meant exactly that, and used in

Scottish Law, by a majority of 13-2. The suggestions of Pierre taking his own life or accidentally overdosing, could not be ruled out, so she received the benefit of the doubt.

The ensuing scandal resulted in her marriage to William Minnoch being cancelled. Soon afterwards she went and stayed with a relative, in Scaldwell in Northamptonshire. He was the local vicar and her ghost is supposed to haunt the churchyard. Nobody can explain why, as she died and was buried in America.

In due course she married George Wardle. Her father attended the wedding, and gave her a handsome settlement but, apparently excluded her from his will. Interestingly, Wardle was the manager for William Morris of the **Arts and Crafts Movement**. The Morris family made some of their money from arsenic, which was in great demand for paint and other decorative purposes as well as patent medicines.

Through George, Madeleine became involved in the **pre-Raphaelite Brotherhood**, which included people like Dante Gabriel Rossetti, John Everett Millais and William Holman Hunt. Their marriage did not last because George found her too domineering and would not want to upset her too much in case she interfered with his food. Her son Tom became a socialist, and her daughter, called Kitten, shocked society by smoking in public!!

Some of Madeleine's letters disappeared after the trial, and a clerk in the Judiciary Office was later imprisoned for stealing them. The writer George Eliot described her as '*being one of the least fascinating of murderesses.*' Madeleine died at the age of ninety-three.

The question remains unanswered. How was Pierre poisoned? Suicide and accidental death cannot be ruled out as he was believed to be an arsenic eater: neither can murder. But, if it was the latter, how did she, or somebody else do it?

If he was murdered, then Madeleine has to be number one suspect. They may well have met on the night Pierre died, and there was a suggestion she gave him a cup of cocoa. If so, it could have contained the arsenic, described as being enough to kill forty people. Remember, arsenic is tasteless.

The other suggestion, far too delicate for Victorian ears, is that Pierre took the arsenic when he indulged in oral sex with her. If that was so, had she deliberately set out to poison him, or had it been a sexual game which went tragically wrong? Had he taken the arsenic to improve his sexual prowess but overdosed in the process? Could it have been a combination of the two activities? Certainly, their sexual activity might have been why Pierre would not tell his landlady what he had been doing.

Although a Presbyterian, Madeleine paid for Masses to be said for Pierre for nearly sixty years after his death.

Author's comments

Was Madeleine a wicked woman?

Like many of the characters in this book, this is not a question with a straight-forward answer, especially as she was found not proven as opposed to guilty or not guilty. There can be little doubt she was sexually active, both before and during her engagement to William, but the all-important question remains unanswered. If she poisoned Pierre on the fateful night, how did she do it? Could it have been in the cocoa or was it whilst they engaged in oral sex? The latter would have been almost if not entirely impossible to prove, especially given the Victorian attitudes of the day. We should also remember he was an arsenic eater for the specific purpose of enhancing his sexual performance.

There was very little sympathy for his blackmailing activities, and he can be considered the author of his own misfortune. But do two wrongs make a right?

Madeleine had the motive to stop him causing problems with the letters. She also had the means having previously purchased arsenic, albeit it mixed with soot to avoid any accidents. Being mixed in cocoa would have helped disguise the soot's taste and colour.

Opportunity was the big problem, which cannot be proved.

I think Madeleine was a spoilt child and a wilful individual, who not only wanted, but usually got her own way. But she met her match with Pierre and was that why he was murdered?

Whatever the judge and her defence might have thought about her guilt, the verdicts are the correct ones in law. The Crown has to prove guilt, but the defence does not have to prove innocence.

Back to the question of wickedness. Going by the trial verdict, legally she was innocent and not wicked.

Looking at her lifestyle, she was certainly wilful, headstrong, unconventional and manipulative until she met her match with Pierre. He was also headstrong and wilful and, much more to the point, had possession of the letters which gave him a tremendous advantage. Also, he did not want just money: he wanted much more than that and would not be satisfied with less. Then he conveniently died.

It was just too co-incidental, and policemen, past and present, do not believe in coincidences. He had nothing to gain from suicide. Accidental death cannot be completely ruled out.

My verdict is she was wicked and most likely murdered him either by the cocoa or the oral sex, which is where the Crown's case floundered. Not proven was the correct legal verdict, but, as its very name suggests, not necessarily the true one.

32
Hannah Snell *aka* James Grey (1723-1792)

Although known later as James Grey, Hannah was born in Worcester to Samuel and Mary Snell. The locals who knew her maintained how she regularly played soldiers as a child. This was perhaps unsurprising as her grandfather was a distinguished soldier, and her other eight siblings had either followed in his footsteps or married soldiers. Regardless of how much soldiering she may have had in her blood, unlike today, there was no chance of a female ever joining the army.

Her parents died in 1740 and with nothing to keep her in Worcester, Hannah went to seek her fortune in London. Whilst living with her sister in Wapping, she met and fell in love with a Dutch seaman, James Summs, who she married in 1744. At first all was well, but after seven months of marriage, he disappeared leaving her pregnant.

It was never established why he left her. Possibly he might have returned to sea to avoid his marital responsibilities. Alternatively, he could have been forced into military service, either in the army or by a press gang.

Hannah had her baby, Susannah, who sadly died within the year. Susannah's death now enabled Hannah to mount her own search for James which she carried out in a most unusual manner.

She reasoned if James had been pressed into military service, then she would look in the army for him. Binding her breasts as flat as she could, Hannah borrowed some of her brother-in-law's clothes and dressed in them. Calling herself James Grey, which was his name, she made her way to Coventry, where John Guise's Sixth Regiment of Foot, later the Royal Warwickshire Regiment, was on a recruiting drive. They had only recently returned from the West Indies, where many soldiers had died.

It was late 1745 and Prince Charles Edward Stuart, also known as the Young Pretender, and his **Jacobite** army were advancing through Scotland towards England, in what was known as *The 45 Rebellion*. Panic was rife in England and there was a great need for troops. Hannah hoped she might discover something here about her missing husband.

It is not known if Hannah was tricked or volunteered to enlist, but before leaving Coventry, she had been recruited into Captain Miller's Company and her search was on.

Being in the army guaranteed her a uniform and food, which she would have to pay for, but being a soldier also meant earning money. As an added benefit, she was fulfilling of her lifelong ambition of becoming a soldier. She adapted to military life and quickly had a good knowledge of her weapons and how to use them.

Hannah soon came to the notice of her sergeant called Davis. As the regiment moved into Carlisle, he set about planning to rape a local girl and tried to get Hannah to help him. She declined, so his next move was to practically order her to help him. Instead, Hannah warned the girl who escaped, much to the sergeant's fury and he sought revenge. Using his superior rank, he alleged she had neglected her duty and consequently was sentenced to receive 600 lashes.

As she faced away from the soldiers when exposing her back, Hannah was able to keep her breasts hidden. She received 500 lashes without a whimper. She so impressed her commanding officer he had the remainder of her punishment cancelled.

So far, Hannah had not discovered any information about the missing James, and her position in the regiment received a major setback. She recognized a soldier, albeit in another company, who had known her in Wapping. It could only be a matter of time before her true gender was discovered, and she had few illusions about her future treatment, especially from Sergeant Davis.

Hannah's only option was to desert.

After leaving the army, she went to Portsmouth, still determined to find her missing husband, and joined Frazer's Regiment of Marines still disguised as James Grey. Soon after enlisting, her ship *Swallow* sailed for the East Indies to capture Pondicherry. Here she fought well and killed several Frenchmen, but during the battle was wounded in the legs and by a musket ball in her groin. Whilst she let the ship's surgeon treat her legs, she told them nothing about the groin wound. Hannah extracted the ball herself by using her thumb and finger. Somehow, she avoided any infection.

It is thought these injuries possibly rendered her unfit for any further military service. Alternatively, during this time, she learnt her husband had been executed in Genoa for murder. Whatever the reason, Hannah called a halt to her military service.

Her unit returned to Portsmouth and in London where in 1750 she revealed her true gender and more or less left the active military life, but not quite.

Safely back in England, she appeared on the stage in uniform, marching and singing songs. She even wrote to the Duke of Cumberland, who was head of the army, and claimed a military pension. Hannah also sold her story to the *Gentleman's Magazine.*

Her pension claims were accepted and the Royal Hospital, Chelsea granted her an honourable discharge with a pension of £30 (approximately £3,500 today).

For a while she went back to Wapping and leased an inn called the Female Warrior. She had another two husbands and by 1772 was living in Newbury and then later in the Midlands.

Sadly, her mental condition seriously deteriorated in 1791 and Hannah was admitted to the **Bethlem Hospital**.

Hannah died in February 1792 and is buried in the Old Burial Ground, Royal Hospital, Chelsea.

Author's comments

Was Hannah wicked?

Possibly she might have been considered so by some members of the community. Cross dressing was still considered as something disgraceful. In 1898, just slightly over a hundred years after Hannah's death, during the Klondike Gold Rush, cross dressing remained illegal, yet trousers were far more practical for women working on mining sites. Whatever the view might have been in the eighteenth-century, I do not consider Hannah to be wicked.

Was she wilful?

I think there is no doubt about that and once her mind was set on doing something, nothing would change it, unless she came up with a better idea. It took a great deal of courage for a female to enlist in the eighteenth-century army and navy.

Was she unconventional?

Absolutely, although women fighting alongside men are not unknown, albeit not very common until recently. Perhaps the best-known ones are Queen Boudicca and Joan of Arc who led armies. Remember, Joan was executed for cross dressing, not heresy.

We shall never know if Hannah would have pursued a military career if her husband had not disappeared and we still do not know if he was impressed or just ran away.

33

Edith Jessie Thompson *née* Graydon (1893-1923) and Frederick Edward Francis Bywaters (1902-1923)

Although shown as a pair, we are mainly interested in what happened to Edith.

She married Percy Thompson in 1915 and soon realized it was a big mistake. Whilst she was imaginative and passionate, he was totally boring. To make matters worse, she was an avid reader of cheap romantic novels, which only served to highlight her own boredom.

One day in 1921, Edith met Frederick Edward Francis Bywaters again. He was now a laundry steward on the P&O line of ships and had been at school with her brothers. It was love at first sight for both of them, despite her being married and nine years older than him. Bywaters quickly became a friend of the family, and when Edith suggested to Percy about taking in a lodger, he agreed, looking forward to the extra money.

Bywaters happily moved in as their lodger, when he was on shore leave.

It is unclear how long Bywaters remained there, but following a holiday on the Isle of Wight, he left the Thompson house.

To be fair, Percy probably loved Edith, but in his own way. She earned more money than he did and was far more outgoing. Undoubtedly born before her time, Edith lived in a changing world, where the last bastions of Victorian and Edwardian society, were fighting a hopeless rearguard action against the modern, post war rapidly changing way of life. Edith never realized until too late how this attitude would be her undoing.

Since meeting Bywaters, Edith began to romanticize about him visiting foreign lands and how she could share his life. Even more dangerously, she wrote copious letters to him, often including tracts from some of her latest novels, which were full of passion. Some involved wronged wives and lovers wanting their revenge, and on occasion mentioned poison. The inference, although never substantiated, was they should murder Percy, as he had refused to divorce her.

They had discussed having a divorce, but Percy would not agree and walking out on him was not an option.

Such action might cost her job, for which she was paid £6 per week (approximately £174 today), and would it be worth it? Even if it was, facing the ensuing scandal was something else. Edith did not want to start life with Bywaters in such a way. She clearly wanted him to be her husband and not a secret lover. With the benefit of hindsight, it would have been better if she had carried on with their current arrangement.

Whilst she destroyed the few letters he wrote, Bywaters kept all of hers, despite being asked not to do so. They would be recovered by the police and used in damning evidence against her.

At some stage Percy became fully aware of the situation. Was this why Bywaters left the house on their return from the Isle of Wight? Despite their several quarrels, Edith continued seeing Bywaters, usually on a weekday.

It could not continue in this fashion and matters came to a head.

The lovers met for tea on 3 October 1922, and Edith told Bywaters how Percy was taking her to the theatre that night. They parted but Bywaters became obsessed with the thoughts of his Edith being taken out by Percy and then going back home with him.

He decided it had to end now.

As Edith and Percy walked from Ilford railway station, towards their home in Belgrave Road, Bywaters suddenly appeared. He pushed Edith out of the way, and then struggled with Percy before running off. Percy was left bleeding and lying in the road. By the time help had arrived, it was too late.

He had received nine stab wounds; four slight cuts to his ribs; two superficial cuts on his chin; one on his inner arm; two to his neck, one of which severed his *carotid artery*.

Clearly this was a murder and the police were soon involved. As their enquiries progressed, the tangled *ménage-à-trois* unraveled, helped by their finding all the letters which Edith had written to Bywaters.

Letters which he had not destroyed as requested.

In due course, they were both arrested and charged with Percy's murder.

Their trial opened at the Old Bailey in December and the cards were stacked against Edith from the outset.

Mr Justice Shearman tried the case. He was one of the *Victorian Standards Old Guard* and exercised his right for them to be tried jointly. This action was greatly prejudicial to her case. The inference with the joint trial being she had conspired, with Bywaters to murder her husband.

Edith made matters worse when she insisted, against legal advice, to give sworn evidence, on her own behalf, as she was now entitled to do. As her barrister had warned, once in the witness box, her letters to Bywaters had selected paragraphs read aloud. The jury was left to put its own interpretations on them.

Bernard Henry Spilsbury, later Sir Bernard, the famous forensic pathologist, who was born and educated in Leamington Spa, agreed he had not found any traces of poison in Percy's body. This had been suggested in a paragraph she had written in one of her letters. But the jury was reminded, Edith was not charged with poisoning her husband, but with putting influence on Bywaters to kill him, as per comments she had made in her letters.

Many of the letters talked about her being prepared to wait years for them to be free to marry, hardly indicative of her inciting him to murder Percy. The defence produced witnesses from the scene, who described Edith as being genuinely shocked by what had happened, hardly the reaction of a conspirator.

Her defence of only quoting from the novels she had read, was dismissed almost out of hand. Likewise, so was the poison inference. As no poison had been found in Percy's body, it pointed to her written comments as being just figments of her imagination. And, if that was so, it could be argued the other comments should be treated in the same way. The judge completely dismissed that and other defences in his summing up.

The judge's summing up was incredibly biased against her. He gave no advice to the jury about taking her vivid imagination into account. If that omission was bad, it might have been forgetfulness, but the same cannot be said for his main omission.

There had been a suggestion from the letters how Edith had poisoned Percy either with *arsenic* or more likely *powdered light bulb glass*. A month after the murder, Spilsbury performed an autopsy on Percy's exhumed body. He found no traces of arsenic or powdered glass. Such evidence was vitally important to the defence. Bearing in mind Spilsbury's impeccable reputation and regular court appearances as a Crown witness, there can be no suggestion this latter omission by the judge was anything but deliberate, because it would have helped Edith tremendously.

Both were found guilty and sentenced to death.

Bywaters had always denied she had any pre-knowledge of Percy's death. In his own defence, Bywaters maintained he had tried to reason with Percy, possibly using threats, to divorce Edith. Matters got out of hand and he stabbed Percy, not intending to kill but merely to frighten him. It was pure bad luck one of the stabs severed Percy's carotid artery, which tended to support his version of events. But, if you take a knife to frighten someone, then you may very well intend to use it.

Although their case was referred to the comparatively new Court of Criminal Appeal, the judges fully agreed with the original sentence, describing the affair as '*a squalid and rather indecent case of lust and adultery.*' In the early days, they would have been unlikely to go against the decision of one of their fellow judges. They conveniently ignored the trial judge's omissions.

Edith maintained her innocence to the end. A massive petition for clemency was raised, which was rejected by the then Home Secretary, William Bridgeman, Member of Parliament for Oswestry. He was regarded as weak and being worried about repercussions from the morality groups if he intervened.

They were both executed on the morning of 9 January 1923. Edith was hanged at Holloway by James Ellis. She collapsed and had to be carried to the scaffold and never regained consciousness. Bywaters walked to his execution calmly enough, no doubt guilty, where he was hanged by William Willis.

James Ellis tried to take his own life only a few days later. It was said he, along with many other people, felt Edith had not been fairly tried and was very affected by her execution. In fact, he resigned/retired soon afterwards. In 1931, he succeeded in taking his own life.

It can be said Edith Jessie Thompson was hanged, not for murder, but for adultery. A few years later, it might have been a different outcome. Her execution undoubtedly affected the outcome in the Alma Rattenbury Trial a few years later.

Author's comments

Was Edith wicked?

If people consider adultery to be wicked, then yes: she was. When it came to her trial for murder, I really do not think so. She was undoubtedly a romancer as evidenced by her choice of literature, but in my opinion, that does not make her wicked.

Was Edith wilful?

Undoubtedly, she was strong willed, and if only she had retained her right to silence and not gone into the witness box, things might have been very much different. No doubt she was probably influenced by the Florence Maybrick trial and it might just possibly have worked. But she was up against a system which was determined to make an example of her. Was this why Mr Justice Shearman was chosen to try the case. Being strong willed worked to her disadvantage.

Her defence counsel always maintained he could have won an acquittal had she not gone into the witness box. But Edith was a vain and obstinate woman.

Was she unconventional? Looking at her case in 1922, then she was.

I believe she did not have a fair trial, irrespective of whether she was guilty or not.

Her motive for murdering Percy would be so she could marry Bywaters. Percy would not agree to a divorce. That could be proved or could it? The Crown must have been grateful for the letters to strengthen a weak case. I feel her defence did not do as well as they should have with them.

Why did the defence not concentrate more on the lack of arsenic and powdered glass in Percy's body, which was at odds with one of her letters. Why did the judge not comment? The way Spilsbury's evidence was treated, coupled with the glaring omissions in the summing up, would be good grounds today for a re-trial.

The means had to be Bywaters stabbing Percy. Yet it took him nine attempts before the fatal stroke. On the negative side was the fact he had gone out with a knife. This is very indicative of a pre-meditated crime

His opportunity came when he discovered Edith and Percy were going to the theatre and he laid in wait for them on their return.

Motive, means and opportunity can all be applied to Bywaters whose jealousy wanted Percy out of the way. Only motive can be remotely proved in Edith's case, certainly not means and opportunity.

In fact, her case has been the subject of a recent television programme. The unanimous verdict of all parties was the verdict was unsafe and should be re-visited. Whether it will is another matter.

Meanwhile, Edith's body has at long last been re-interred with her parents, which is a step in the right direction.

I have included Edith's case in this publication for two reasons. Firstly, because I feel her trial was grossly unfair even by the standards of the time: and secondly the evidence just was not there to even justify charging her, let alone going to court. I doubt the evidence would even pass any committal stages today.

Remember, this was 1922, not quite a hundred years ago and Edith was hanged for adultery and not murder.

34
Katherine Webster *née* Lawlor, *aka* Webb, Gibbs, Shannon and Thomas (c1849-1879)

In January 1879, Kate Webster, alias Lawlor, Webb, Gibbs, Shannon and soon to be Thomas plus her young son, lived a precarious existence in London. She had been born in County Wexford, Ireland to respectable parents, but did not follow in their footsteps.

From a very early age, she was a persistent thief and no amount of persuasion from her parents and reinforced by the local priest, could change her. No doubt they a gave a huge sigh of relief when she left home and travelled to Liverpool. It is unclear where Kate obtained the money for her passage, but the general belief was she had stolen it.

However, Kate was not as good at thieving as she thought she was.

During the next few years, she saw the inside of several prison cells. One of her favourite tricks was to obtain lodgings in a boarding house, then when the opportunity arose, she sold off as many of the removable items from there, as she could. Somewhere along the line, she acquired a son.

In early 1879, she depended entirely on the charity of Sarah Crease, who found her work as a domestic servant for Mrs Martha Julia Thomas, a wealthy widow who lived in Park Road, Richmond, Surrey. It is believed Kate left her son with Sarah or else abandoned him somewhere in London.

By late February, Mrs Thomas was not prepared to employ her for very much longer. Kate spent much of her time in the nearby pub, The Hole in the Wall, and neglected her work. On Sunday 2 March 1879, Mrs Thomas gave her one month's notice, and went to church, leaving a cursing Kate behind.

When she returned, Mrs Thomas entered her house and was never seen alive again.

Furious about being given notice, Kate flew at her employer with a meat cleaver as she entered the house. Mrs Thomas stood no chance.

After having killed her mistress, Kate set about dismembering the body, and boiling up the pieces in a large copper cauldron. With the occasional refreshment break at The Hole in the Wall, Kate worked all through the night to dispose of the body and burn the bones. The stench must have been vile, but Kate's idea was to destroy any remains of Martha Thomas and make whatever was left unrecognizable as even being human.

It is at this point when Kate entered the realms of real infamy.

As she boiled up Martha's body, a layer of fat kept appearing on the surface of the water. Kate scraped this off and later, so it has been said, sold it as first class dripping to The Hole in the Wall. Later historians have denied this legend, so, it may have or may not have happened. Nevertheless, it guaranteed Kate immortal infamy.

On Tuesday morning, Kate pawned Martha's gold false teeth for £6 (approximately £390 today). Then, wearing her late employer's jewellery and one of her dresses, Kate, now calling herself Mrs Thomas arranged for a Mr Porter to buy the furniture from the house.

Meanwhile, she had disposed of some heavy boxes into the Thames.

Henry Wheatley, discovered one of them, floating in the river, the next day. Thinking there might be something valuable in it, or perhaps a reward for its return, he brought it ashore. His hopes quickly vanished when he opened it and found some cooked human remains inside. He called the police.

Several days, later removal man John Church, arrived as arranged, at Martha's house and began loading the dead woman's belongings.

After their first meeting, John had been going out with Kate, never suspecting he was being taken for a ride. To make matters worse for him, Martha's next door neighbours became suspicious. They had been concerned at not having seen Martha for some days and informed the police. Church was arrested but Kate escaped.

But not for long.

Her freedom ended when she was arrested ten days later at Killane, County Wexford, in Ireland, still wearing Martha's dress and jewellery. By then the police had searched Martha's cottage and found some human bones. The connection was soon made with the remains found in the box and others in the Thames, although Martha's head remained missing.

Whilst in custody, Kate tried to blame everyone she came across for killing Martha, but it was to no avail and in due course, she stood trial for murder at the Old Bailey. It was a complicated case, and her defence, as instructed, tried to put the blame onto John Church and next-door neighbor Henry Porter. Nevertheless, the jury found her guilty. Even after they delivered their verdict and before being sentenced to death, she still claimed her innocence and fought the verdict by pleading she was pregnant. The case was adjourned whilst this was checked out. They were yet more lies and sentence of death followed.

There were some attempts made to have her death sentence commuted to life imprisonment, despite the heinousness of her crime, but nobody listened.

On 29 July 1879, she was hanged at Wandsworth prison by William Marwood, after cursing him. However, she had made a full confession the night before.

She gained very little from this crime.

Not too long ago, a skull was found near the house in a garden which belongs to Sir David Attenborough. It is thought this could be Martha's missing head.

Author's comments

Was Kate Webster, or whatever other name you like to call her, a wicked woman?

I think there is very little doubt she was. Irrespective of her criminal background, this was a cold premeditated act. She planned it and waited for Martha to come back from church before she struck. Had Martha not given her notice would the murder still have occurred? Possibly not.

Her motive in murdering Martha was revenge for being dismissed. Kate could just as easily have robbed her without committing murder. The means were with the meat cleaver which must have made quite a mess, not only of Martha and there would have been a considerable amount of blood. Opportunity was not difficult to prove as she had lain in wait for Martha to return and then attacked her.

All her actions were pre-meditated.

There is also the tale about her selling off Martha's body fat at The Hole in the Wall. If, and I stress if, it was true, then it was a wicked act for which there can be no excuse. No doubt it would have amused Kate, but there is some doubt as to the truth of this story.

Was she wilful?

I think there can be no doubt. She was only interested in herself. Her whole, albeit short life, involved taking advantage of opportunities as they presented themselves.

Was she unconventional?

Undoubtedly, but this fades into insignificance with Martha's murder.

Kate Webster was a cold and callous murderer, who had no compassion or compunction when it came to furthering herself. I can find nothing to say in her favour except for making a full confession on the eve of her execution.

Glossary

Acqua Tofana
A slow-acting, strong poison used mainly in Italy and sold as a cosmetic. It was a mixture of arsenic, lead and possibly belladonna. Being tasteless and colourless, it was easily mixed with water and wine.

Amoebic dysentery
A serious infection of the intestines caused by swallowing or eating contaminated water or food.

Antimony and Tartar emetic
Was used for conditioning horses and found in most stables. Tartar emetic is a derivative of antimony and a very painful poison.

Arsenic
A popular white powder poison used for killing pests and also cosmetic purposes. Being coloured white it had to be mixed with either a dye or soot, when sold to ensure it was not mistaken for sugar, flour or other similar white coloured products.

It is a natural element commonly found as impurities in metal ores. As a murderer's weapon, arsenic has been used for hundreds of years and remained popular in Victorian times, mainly because it was difficult to detect and easy to obtain. Symptoms, such as vomiting, or stomach pains, made it a great imitator making a diagnosis of gastric fever more likely, and a death being recorded as natural causes.

From a sadistic murderer's point of view, arsenic caused an exceptionally painful death, if revenge was wanted. It gradually ceased to be used for murdering people as advances in forensic science made it easier to detect in bodies.

As early as 1836, it was discovered how arsenic remained in the body for a long time, after death. Twenty years later, this did not cause too much of a problem as the Victorians were masters of the art of mournful funerals, with all the trappings. As such, exhumations were unthinkable without fully justified suspicions. Should an autopsy be necessary, it had to be done very quickly or run the risk of not happening at all.

If taken in the right quantities, it was a sexual stimulant, probably along the lines that *viagra* is used today. cases. It gradually ceased to be used as forensic science improved and made it easier to discover in bodies. Sometimes known as *'Inheritance Powder'* it could be sprinkled over an ailing relative's food to speed up their demise and inheritance!

Arsenica
A homeopathic remedy with a multitude of uses.

Arts and Crafts Movement
Founded in mid-nineteenth century Britain to replace the then current design and decoration as a protest against mechanical and factory-produced goods.

Astral projection
Briefly, an intentional out of body experience.

Asymptomatic carrier
A person who has been infected with a disease but shows no sign of any infections and passes it on to other people.

Autopsy
Also known as a **postmortem**. The full examination of a dead body to ascertain cause of death and for educational purposes.

Bethlem Hospital aka Bethlehem Hospital and Bedlam

This hospital first admitted patients with mental problems in 1377. As the years passed it became known as Bedlam and scandalously exposed mentally affected patients to public view.

Bicarbonate of soda

Also known as sodium bicarbonate, it is a compound for combatting stomach ache.

Broadmoor Criminal Lunatic Asylum

A high security psychiatric hospital in Crowthorne, Berkshire, for the criminally insane. It opened in 1863 and is a hospital, not a prison.

Bubonic plague

A fatal disease, usually started when people were infected with rat fleas, becoming highly contagious via touch or from other people coughing or sneezing. Choosing Bubonic Plague as a cause of death would certainly stop any enquiry in its tracks. Even with antibiotics today, it has a ten percent fatality rate. It would have been much worse in Mary Bateman's day.

Burial clubs

Friendly Societies collecting weekly payments to ensure members received a proper funeral and burial. First recorded in Ancient Rome and ancestor of modern funeral plans.

Carotid artery

Situated on either side of the throat for conveying oxygenated blood to the brain.

Chloroform

Discovered in 1831, it was not introduced into medicine until 1847. A colourless liquid, half as heavy again as water and made by distilling alcohol with slaked lime and chloride of lime. It was used as an anaesthetic. Small doses may be taken orally for relieving sickness and headaches. However, if taken in large doses is a violent irritant and poison.

Chloride of lime
A white powder used for disinfectant purposes when mixed with slaked lime and chloride.

Cholera
See English cholera.

Circumstantial evidence
Is inferred evidence with more than one possible explanation. It must be corroborated to remove any reasonable doubt.

Clairvoyant
The ability to gain information about people or things etc by extrasensory perception.

Cocaine
A highly addictive recreational drug made from coca leaves from South America

Coeliac disease
An auto-immune disease caused by an abnormal reaction to gluten.

Corrosive sublimate
A white poisonous soluble crystalline sublimate of mercury. It had several uses including being an anti-septic. Once used to treat *syphilis*, now discontinued because of its toxic mercury content and better medicines being available. It is very toxic to humans who can take up to a fortnight to die depending on the quantity ingested. Symptoms include serious internal damage, stomach pains and ulcers.

Criminal conversation
A common law matter arising from adultery in a marriage and is another recognized term for sexual intercourse or anything which interfered with a married couple. Only a husband could sue for a breach of fidelity and the other man was the sole defendant. This law decreed the wife, husband and

defendant were not permitted to testify. The evidence was obtained from other witnesses, such as servants.

The stakes were high and could cost the adulterer in the region of £10,000-£20,000 damages (well into millions of pounds today). It was abolished in England during 1851, but still exists in some American States.

Defence of the Realm Act 1914, aka D.O.R.A
This was emergency legislation enacted within hours of the First World War starting and exercised all manner of draconian powers and restrictions.

Dermatitis Herpetiformis
A chronic auto-immune skin blistering condition first detected as such in 1884. Jean-Paul Marat probably suffered from it and could only find relief in a bathtub of herb infused water, which was where he conducted his business. Coeliac is an offshoot of this disease.

Dogcart
A horse drawn vehicle designed for carrying retrieving dogs for shooters. Developed into carrying humans.

Dyspepsia
Indigestion.

Epsom Salts
Also known as magnesium sulphate, used for soothing aching joints, skin infections and constipation.

Eczema
Inflamed, itchy or flaking skin.

English cholera
An often fatal infection of the small intestine, caused by poor sanitation and drinking infected water. It is only contracted by humans and symptoms include severe diarrhoea leading to chronic dehydration.

Between 1846 and 1860, England was infected by a world-wide pandemic, which was referred to as English cholera. This was a vague term given to any kind of disease which was accompanied by diarrhoea.

French Revolution
1789-1799 began with the storming of the Bastille and finished when Napoleon seized power. A very violent period in France's history involving the overthrow and execution of the monarchy. See also Reign of Terror.

Gastric fever
An old name for typhoid fever.

Gastritis
An inflammation of the stomach.

Gastroenteritis
Infectious diarrhoea with various causes such as virus, bacteria etc. Often called a stomach bug.

Girondins
A loosely knit political faction and not really a party as such although active in the French National Assembly. Less radical than the Jacobins, they believed Louis XVI should not be executed and favoured war against other countries to bring the French Nation together. The Jacobins (see below) were very intolerant towards them.

Grand Tour
Regarded as the young nobleman's rite of passage when he took a long tour through Europe to improve his general education. It was expensive and only undertaken by people whose family had plenty of money. Young men from other countries followed suit, but it was more of an English activity than other nationalities.

Humours
Liquids within the human body identified as blood, phlegm, black bile and yellow bile and associated with air, water, fire and earth. First suggested circa

540-500BC and later studied by Hippocrates.

Hydrocyanic acid
See Prussic acid.

Hydrotherapy
An alternative medical treatment using water that was very popular in Malvern.

Hypochondriac
Someone who has a fear of having serious undiagnosed ailments.

Iphigenia
She was the daughter of King Agamemnon who offended the goddess Artemis during the Trojan War. The only way Agamemnon could appease Artemis was to sacrifice his daughter to her. He did so in one version, but in another she was rescued.

Jacobins
Created by Maxmilien Roberspierre in 1789 during the French Revolution and originally known as *The Society of Friends of the Constitution.* Later changed to *The Society of Jacobin Friends of Freedom and Equality in Government.* They were known as Jacobins and advocated extreme violence against anybody who opposed their views. Their name came from the Jacobin convent near the National Assembly where they were formed.

Jacobites
Followers of the exiled King James II of England and his descendants.

Jactitation suit
Used when someone boasted about being married when they were not. The main party prayed for the other to keep quiet and not make any more such boasts. Only the boaster could contest the issue by denying ever having made the boast if it was true, or there was an allegation the petitioner had agreed to the boasts being made.

Jointure
Financial provision made by a husband for his wife on his death, provided she had not been responsible for it.

Laudanum
Another name for tincture of opium.

Laurel water
Contained a small quantity of hydrocyanic acid and used for soothing solutions.

Malaria
A disease caused by certain parasites in the blood.

Married Womens Property Acts 1870 & 1882
Initially gave women the right to keep the money they earned and to inherit property. Later Act included owning their own property,

Medical creosote
A distillation of tars used mainly as an antiseptic. If ingested, would cause acidic burning in the mouth and severe stomach pains. Consequently, it was for external use only and not for ingesting.

Ménage-à-trois
Arrangement whereby a married couple have a lover living with them.

Mercuric chloride
A mixture of mercury and chlorine which is very toxic to humans.

Mercury
A heavy fluid metal which is a strong antiseptic and used as purgatives and treatment of syphilis. Continued taking of mercury can result in being poisoned, resulting in death if not stopped.

National Society for the Prevention of Cruelty to Children. (NSPCC)
Formed to protect children in 1884. Granted permission in 1895 to use title Royal but decided to retain National, which was widely recognized, believing change of name would cause confusion.

Necrosis
A serious bone decaying disease.

Neuralgia
A nerve pain.

Nux Vomica
Useful as a tonic but poisonous in large quantities.

Nymphomaniac
A woman who is addicted to sex.

Opium
Dried juice of unripe seed capsules of the white Indian poppy and a valuable medicament. See also Laudanum.

Petty treason
Petty Treason or Petit Treason was a Common Law Offence (derived from custom or legal precedent: not by statute). Regarded as more serious than murder, with only High Treason being the greatest crime in the land, which is why it used to have very severe and harsh penalties.

Committed by a servant who murdered their master and/or mistress and by a wife who murdered her husband, (but not by a husband who murdered his wife). The penalty of being burnt alive at the stake was last practised in 1797 and replaced by hanging. This offence fell into disuse and was finally repealed in 1828.

Philtre
A love potion.

Phossy Jaw
Necrosis of the jaw caused by contact with white phosphorus.

Pneumonia
Serious inflammation of the lungs.

Postmortem
See Autopsy.

Powdered light bulb glass
Once believed to be a poison but disproved in recent years.

Pre-Raphaelite Brotherhood
Formed in 1884 and aimed at reforming art by rejecting the approach commonly adopted by current artists. They aimed to return to the style of art which existed before Raphael Sanzio 1483-1520. He was the acclaimed Italian artist of the High Renaissance. This new brotherhood included artists such as Dante Gabriel Rosetti, John Everett Millais and William Holman Hunt.

Press gangs
The practice of impressment had been in existence for centuries and consisted of forcibly abducting men into military service. 1744 saw the beginning of almost unabated wars against the French until 1815, which meant a continuous need for soldiers and sailors. Forcible impressment for soldiers was banned in 1780, but for the navy would not fall into disuse until post 1815. Press gangs made no distinction between nationalities and religion.

Prussic acid
Also known as hydrocyanic acid is a very deadly poison with a pleasant smell and taste. Acts rapidly in paralyzing the nervous system with death resulting in minutes or even seconds.

Pulmonary tuberculosis
A disease which mainly invades the lungs sometimes known as consumption.

Quack remedies
Remedies which are not believed to work as they have not been scientifically proved. Sold and prescribed by quack doctors.

Quicklime
Believed to speed up decay of bodies although disputed by some, claiming the opposite effect.

Reincarnation
A new life after death.

Reign of Terror
Ran in France from 5 September 1793-28 July to 1794 during the French Revolution and aimed at removing anybody who was or could be possibly seen as an enemy of the State. More than 16,000 people were executed during the period, Robespierre was one of the main leaders.

Schizophrenia
A mental condition whereby an afflicted person has a second personality.

South Sea Bubble Affair
The South Sea Company began in 1711, had a trade monopoly with South America. It offered, in 1719, to take over half the national debt for further concessions. A huge speculation followed but the bubble finally burst in 1720 and many thousands of people were ruined. Financial confidence was finally restored by Robert Walpole when he became prime minister.

Strychnine
An alkaloid derived from nux vomica with a very bitter taste. Can be beneficial in very small doses as a stimulant but is a dangerous drug in larger quantities.

Syphilis
A contagious sexually transmitted disease, once known as the French Pox.

Tartar emetic
See Antimony.

Theosophy
A religion whereby knowledge of God may be achieved by spiritual ecstasy and other means.

Typhoid
An often fatal disease first recorded in 460BC, caused by salmonella typhi, and continued ever since. Vaccines first appeared in the late nineteenth century and were not publicly available in America until 1914. They had been used experimentally on the military in 1896.

Symptoms range from poor appetite, acute abdominal pain, headaches, fever, coughing and internal bleeding, also some discolouring of the skin. Early treatments could not be guaranteed to work and were aimed at reducing the fever side of the disease.

When contaminated water and food were identified as the main causes, it became very important for the patient to avoid them. If this course of action was followed, there was a reasonable chance of the patient recovering.

Once antibiotics appeared, they quickly controlled the disease. Unfortunately, today typhoid is becoming more and more resistant to antibiotics. Its main causes remain the same: consuming contaminated water and food, with the most common method of spreading being via urine and faeces from someone who had the disease, or as in Mallon's case, a carrier.

For anyone involved in the handling of food, it was vitally important they washed their hands regularly, especially after urinating or defecating. This is something we tend to take for granted today, but food handlers do need reminding.

Typhoid can only be spread by humans to other humans. Animals are not affected.

Viagra
Used to treat erectile dysfunction in men and much safer than taking arsenic.

Voyeur

A person who gets sexual pleasure from watching naked people or persons who are engaging in sexual activity.

Wake

A day set aside to celebrate the patronal saint of the local church. Parishioners would watch in their church overnight (aka watching or waking) prior to the feasting and games etc the following day.

Whooping cough aka Pertussis

This is a highly infectious bacterial infection of the lungs, more commonly known as whooping cough from the sounds that can accompany a coughing fit. The bacterium tends to die off after three weeks and antiobiotics may not work.

Acknowledgements and Further Reading

Billingham, Nick, *Foul Deeds & Suspicious Deaths in Stratford & South Warwickshire*

Birkenhead, The First Earl of, Frederick Edwin Smith, *Famous Trials*

Blyth, Henry, *Madeleine Smith: A Famous Victorian Murder Trial*

Bolitho, Paul, *Ripples from Warwickshire's Past*

Bolitho, Paul, *More Ripples from Warwickshire's Past*

Bondeson, Jon, *Victorian Murders*

Bridges, Yseult, *How Charles Bravo Died*

Browne, Douglas G and Tullet Tom, *Bernard Spilsbury*

Burton, Sarah, *Imposters*

Campbell, Jimmy Powdrell, *A Scottish Murder Rewriting the Madeleine Smith Story*

Canwell, Diane, *Women Who Shook the Nation*

Colquhon Kate, *Did She Kill Him?*

Comrie, John D, *Black's Medical Dictionary*

Cordingley, David, *Heroines and Harlots*

Diamond Michael, *Victorian Sensation*

Emsley, John, *The Elements of Murder*

Franklin, Charles, *World Famous Acquittals*

Gardiner, Juliet, *Who's Who in British History*

Goodman, Jonathan, *Medical Murders*

Green, Jonathon, *The Directory of Infamy*

Griffiths, Arthur, *The Chronicles of Newgate*

Griffiths, Arthur, *Mysteries of Police and Crime*
Hall, Angus, *Crimes of Horror*
Hamilton, Elizabeth, *The Warwickshire Scandal*
Harrison, Shirley, *The Diary of Jack the Ripper*
Hartman. Mary S, *Victorian Murderesses*
Honeycombe, Gordon, *The Murders of the Black Museum 1870-1970*
Hutchinson Factfinder
Hutchinson's Encyclopedia of Britain
JL Publishing, *Chronicle of Britain and Ireland*
Johnson Keith, *Tales of Old Lancashire*
Johnson, W H, *Surrey Murder Case Book*
Lane, Brian, *The Murder Guide*
Lewis, Roy Harley, *Victorian Murders*
Macdonald & Evans, *A Dictionary of Law*
Macnair, Miles, *Olive Princess of Cumberland, a Royal Scandal*
Magazine Articles
Mortimer QC, John, *Famous Trials*
Napley, Sir David, *Murder at the Villa Madeira*
O'Connor, Sean, *The Fatal Passion of Alma Rattenbury*
Parrish J M & Crossland, John R, *The Fifty Most Amazing Crimes of the last 100 Years*
Parry, David, *Lady Poisoners*
Pipe, Marian & Butler, Mia, *Walks in Mysterious Northamptonshire*
Ruddick, James, *Death at the Priory*
Ryan, Bernard, *The Poisoned Life of Mrs Maybrick*
Simpson J & S Roud, *Oxford Dictionary of English Folklore*
Smith, Betty, *Tales of Old Stratford*
Strevens, Summer, *First Forensic Hanging*
Sutherland, Graham, *Bloody British History – Warwick*
Sutherland, Graham, *Dastardly Deeds in Victorian Warwickshire*
Sutherland, Graham, *Feisty Females*
Sutherland, Graham, *North to Alaska*
Sutherland, Graham, *Warwickshire Crimes and Criminals*
Sutherland, Graham, *Wicked Women*
Taylor M B. & Wilkinson V L, *Badges of Office*

INDEX

Ettington Sensation, 46
Female Coterie, 97
Fruits of Philosophy, 27-8
Gentleman's Magazine, 198
Hanging Wood, 37
Letters of Junius, 183, 187
Man Who Never Was, 180
Scandalous Lady W, 98
Spectator, 63
Warwickshire Scandal, 167
Westminster Review, 90-91

LEGAL

Crimes, Courts,
Procedures & Legislation etc
Abortion, 49-50
Accessory to Murder, 13
Anonymous Letter Writing, 49, 85-6, 119-23,
Assassination, 133
Assault, 133, 136-9, 158
Attempt Murder, 58-61, 140-44, 153, 164, 192
Autopsy, *see* Postmortem,
Bigamy, 69, 128-9
Blackmail, 109, 117, 128, 190-1, 194-5
Bribery, 120
Burglary, 183-4, 187
Courts,
   Appeal, Court of Criminal,
   London, 2, 60, 166, 180, 203
   Chelmsford, Essex, 58
   Consistory, 127, 129

County, 65
Coventry, Warwickshire, 6
Durham, 70-1
Edinburgh High Court, 192-3
House of Lords, 34, 128, 171
Lewes, Sussex, 86, 101-02,
Liverpool, Lancashire,24, 161-3
Old Bailey, London, 13-14, 86,
152-3, 179-80, 202-3, 208
Oxford, 36
Paris, 76, 80
Unspecified, 28, 120
Warwick, 42-4, 121-22, 132-4,
137-8, 142-3
York, 20
Criminal Conversation, 96
Criminal Lunatics Act 1800, 133
Cross Dressing, 199
Deception, 13, 17-21, 69, 75, 152,
183,186
Defence of the Realm Act (DORA)
1914, 107-08
Execution, 5, 7, 21, 24-5, 37, 59, 61,
71, 74, 77, 80-81, 102, 132-4, 144,
153, 164, 182-3, 187, 182, 203-05,
208-09
Exhumation, 24, 57-8 70, 101, 161
192, 203
Extradition, 37, 76, 78
Gunpowder Plot, 2
Heresy, 199
Hoard Food, 66-7
Incest, 73, 186
Inquest, 12-13, 18,53, 85, 101
Jactitation Suit, 127-8

MEDICAL

227